CLEARLY SOCIAL STUDIES

Grade 5

Author: Marsha Elyn Wright
Editors: Stephanie Garcia, Bob Newman
Cover Designer: Anthony D. Paular
Interior Designer: Anthony D. Paular
Interior Artist: Tani Brooks Johnson

Frank Schaffer Publications®

Judy/Instructo is an imprint of Frank Schaffer Publications.

Send all inquiries to:
Frank Schaffer Publications
3195 Wilson Drive NW
Grand Rapids, Michigan 49544

ISBN: 0-7682-0633-2

3 4 5 6 7 8 9 10 11 MAZ 10 09 08 07 06 05 04

TABLE OF CONTENTS

INTRODUCTION

Clearly Social Studies is designed to help your students develop an understanding of basic social studies concepts taught in fifth grade—how the United States developed; the routes of early explorers and the trails of pioneers heading West; the effects of colonial growth and expansion; different viewpoints during the quest for independence; the promises of the Declaration of Independence and the people involved in building the dream of a new nation; and looking to the future of America. Focus areas of study complement the NCSS (National Council for the Social Studies) *Curriculum Standards for Social Studies*.

Clearly Social Studies encourages the students to broaden their sense of self. The students will begin to connect with the world around them and the people and events that have made a difference in history. Questions are provided, both in the activities and on the reproducibles, that can be used as springboards for rich classroom discussions. The activities in **Clearly Social Studies** help the students apply their skills and knowledge in a variety of formats and presentations. These activities can be used all year to captivate students and enrich your social studies instruction!

Clearly Social Studies content areas of study are separated into different strands featuring art and hands-on, concept-building activities as well as several reproducibles. As an added bonus, **Clearly Social Studies** features a collection of *full-color transparencies* for use throughout the book. Use the transparencies as is, or duplicate and distribute them to the students. Activities designed for use with specific transparencies are marked accordingly. With these transparencies, you are all set for a successful lesson that requires little preparation time for you!

Clearly Social Studies contains bulletin board display ideas and activities to enhance each unit of study. These are featured and described at the beginning of each unit. Each display is designed to be created by both you and your students for a cooperative effort.

Clearly Social Studies can begin with the motivational bulletin board display described below!

Student self-portrait as a tall tale hero and original tall tale

Post a United States map on a wall or bulletin board. Tell the students that a special type of folklore called *tall tales* grew up out of the stories of pioneers settling the North American frontier. These tall tales were based on real stories, but the truth was exaggerated each time the story was told! Read aloud to your students some tall tales about Mike Fink, Paul Bunyan, Slewfoot Sue, Davy Crockett, Sally Ann Thunder, Ann Whirlwind Crockett, and others. Have each student choose a state and write and illustrate a tall tale about an adventure in that state, using himself or herself as the tall tale hero. Remind the students to exaggerate! Have the students practice reading their tales dramatically before reading them to the class. Post the stories around the map. Attach a length of yarn from the story to its "state of origin."

BEFORE COLUMBUS

Help your students understand that before Christopher Columbus sailed to North America, this country was home to millions of people.

Learning About Native Americans

Transparency 1

Begin your study of early America by by asking your students what they know about Native Amerans. List the information on chart paper. Then read to your students some books such as the following:

- *People of the Breaking Day* by Marcia Sewall (Atheneum, 1990)

- *Buffalo Hunt* by Russell Freedman (Holiday House, 1988)

- *Cherokee Summer* by Diane Hoyt-Goldsmith (Holiday House, 1993)

- *Totem Pole* by Diane Hoyt-Goldsmith (Holiday House, 1990)

At the end of your study, read through your list and mark **T** for *true* and **F** for *false* beside each item. Talk about how much of your students' prior knowledge was on target.

Display Transparency 1, *Native American Cultural Groups, U.S. 1500's.* Discuss the different Native American groups shown on the map. Have the students locate their home state to see which group had lived in the area. Ask questions such as *Which group is the largest? Which groups lived in a harsh climate? Which groups probably ate a diet of fish? Which groups probably built their homes from trees?* Challenge the students to ask their own questions to the rest of the class.

"Wampum" Necklaces

Share with your students that wampum were beads carved from white and purple quahog (clam) shells found along the Atlantic shores by many of the Northeastern tribes in the United States. Explain that these beads were polished and strung together in patterns that told a message. Tell the students that wampum was used for belts, jewelry, and money. Have each student make a patterned necklace out of colored macaroni by following the directions below.

Materials:

- container of water
- red and blue food coloring
- quart-size resealable plastic bag
- macaroni
- string or cord
- newspaper
- scissors

Directions:

1. Put about a cup of macaroni in a resealable bag. Add about two teaspoons of water and a few drops of red and blue food coloring to make the color purple.
2. Spread out newspaper over your work space. Shake the bag to mix the food coloring and macaroni. Pour the macaroni onto the newspaper to dry.
3. Cut two or three lengths of string for a necklace.
4. Slide plain macaroni and purple macaroni onto each string in a pattern to make your necklace. When all your strands are "beaded," tie the ends together for a necklace!

One Gigantic Totem Pole

Explain to the students that Northwest Coast tribes carved and painted totem poles to honor people and chronicle legends. Have the students make a class totem pole. Ask the manager of a local ice cream store to save you the empty containers. Give every two students one container. If possible, display pictures of totem poles so that the students learn which animals were most often used—eagle, wolf, salmon, raven, frog, beaver, bear, snake, thunderbird, and whale. Have each pair of students create an animal on a piece of construction paper that has been trimmed to wrap completely around a container. Have the students color their designs with markers; then glue them on the containers. Stack the finished containers to create your very own classroom totem pole!

Ring Toss Game

Tell the students that Northwest Coast children played a ring toss game. Explain that a player tossed rings made out of salmon bones into the air and tried to catch them on a stick. Have the students play a version of this game. Place your students in small groups. Give each group an empty paper towel tube, a length of cord, a one-foot dowel, and scissors. Have each group cut its tube into several one-inch rings, slide the cord through each ring, and tie it on the last ring. Have each group tie the other end of the cord to the dowel. Explain these rules:

The first player holds the "stick" with one hand, tosses the rings up, and tries to catch them onto the stick. The group counts the rings on the stick. The player gets one point for each ring he or she caught. This player gets two more turns. Then it's the next player's turn. At the end of the game, the player with the most points wins!

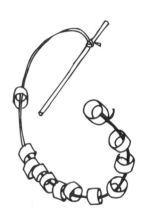

Child's "winter count" artwork

brown mailing paper

Explain to the students that the Lakota Sioux who lived in the Great Plains kept track of the years by "winter counts." Tell the students that every winter the Lakota had an artist record an important event by drawing a picture or symbol of it on an animal hide. List with your students some of the important events in their lives, such as losing a tooth or buying a pet. Give each student a large piece of brown mailing paper, and have him or her tear it around the edges so that it resembles an animal hide. Let the students use bright-colored crayons or markers to draw their important events on the paper. Tell the students to wad up their drawings when they are finished so that the paper wrinkles. Have the students smooth out their drawings and paint over them with a thin wash of watered-down brown tempera paint. Let the students take turns describing their winter counts with the rest of the class. Display the "hides" on a bulletin board.

Coming to the Americas

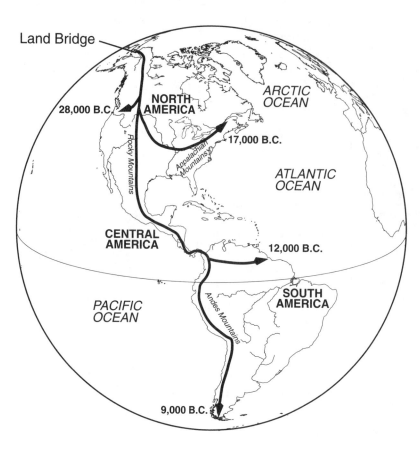

Thousands of years ago, about a third of the earth was covered by glaciers. A **glacier** is a huge sheet of ice. During that time, a strip of land connected Asia and North America across the Bering Strait. Scientists think that people and animals migrated over this land bridge in search of food. **Migrate** means to move from one area to another. These hunters were the ancestors of American Indians. **Ancestors** are relatives who lived before you. When the climate warmed up, the glaciers melted, the seas rose, and water covered the land bridge.

This map shows the paths these first Americans traveled.

Use the map to answer the questions.

1. *B.C.* stands for the time before Christ was born. The larger the number, the earlier the date. Look at the map. To what area did the first people migrate—northwestern North America or northeastern North America? How do you know?

   _____

   _____

2. How many years are there between the time it took people to migrate to northern South America and southern South America? Show your work.

   _____

3. After people first entered the Americas, how long did it take for people to reach the tip of South America? Show your work.

   _____

Two Different Cultures

Don't think that all American Indians are the same. They're not! Many Indians do share the same beliefs, but as they migrated to different regions in North America, they developed different ways of life. The land and its climate effected the kind of food the people ate, the kind of homes they built, and the kind of clothing they wore. Read about two Indian cultures—Northwest Coast and the Southwest.

Northwest Coast

We live by the Pacific Ocean. The sea gives us food. We hunt seals, shellfish, and whales and search for seabird eggs. We use fish oil to light our torches at night. We catch salmon in our many rivers. There is a thick forest of tall cedar trees near our village. We carve the cedar into long canoes that look like giant animals. Some of our canoes are over 50 feet long! We also carve and paint tall cedar totem poles to honor our families and chief. When it rains in winter, we live together in long houses with many families. We tell our children stories in song. Sometimes we have a potlatch ceremony. We eat, sing, and dance for many days.

Southwest

We live near a canyon. The land is very dry. We are farmers. We grow corn with very long roots to drink up the underground water. We collect rainwater and dig ditches to move the water to our crops. We live in pueblos made of clay. A **pueblo** looks like many small houses built together. We get the clay, called **adobe**, from the earth. It keeps our pueblos cool inside when the outside temperature reaches 120°! Some of us make beautiful pottery. Sometimes we have a kachina ceremony. **Kachina** are spirits of the dead who take the form of plants, animals, and humans. Kachina dancers give the children wooden dolls dressed as kachina spirits.

Decide which group each phrase describes. Write **NW** for Northwest Coast, **SW** for Southwest, or **both**. Then turn over this paper. Write how you think these groups are similar.

_____ 1. lived in clay houses

_____ 2. had potlatches

_____ 3. carved totem poles

_____ 4. held ceremonies

_____ 5. had kachina dancers

_____ 6. rainy winters

_____ 7. hunted whales

_____ 8. grew corn

_____ 9. farmers

_____ 10. hunters

People of the Great Plains

Read the information. Then answer the questions.

Most of the Plains Indians were hunters who moved with the seasons. In summer, they roamed the grasslands hunting buffalo. In winter, they hunted in the forests. At first, they walked. Their trained dogs pulled supplies on a **travois** (truh VOY). A travois is like a sled. While they hunted, they lived in portable homes called **tepees**. The tepees were made from animal hides and kept them cool in summer and warm in winter. When Spanish explorers brought horses to America, many runaway horses roamed the Great Plains. The Plains Indians learned to tame these horses and ride them for hunting. They traveled farther and faster!

As explorers and settlers moved west, life for the Plains Indians changed. At first, they peacefully traded with the explorers. But as more Europeans came, so did diseases that the Plains Indians couldn't fight. Many died from smallpox and cholera. Pioneers wanted gold and land. They claimed the Indians' land for themselves. Many Plains Indians banded together to fight back. But soldiers began to attack, killing even peaceful tribes of men, women, and children. The government killed thousands of buffalo herds just to lower the food supply of the Plains Indians. Tribes were forced to live on **reservations**, land set aside for them by the government.

In 1994, a white buffalo calf named Miracle was born. She is the first albino calf to be born in America in 100 years! The white female calf is sacred to the Plains Indians. They believe that the birth of Miracle is a sign of healing for the earth and their people.

1. Why were dogs important to the early people of the Great Plains? _____

   _____

2. How did tepees help the Plains Indians' way of life? _____

   _____

3. How did the horse change the life of the Plains Indians? _____

   _____

4. Why do you think the Indians couldn't fight off the European diseases? _____

   _____

5. Imagine that you are a pioneer. What would you have done if you had met some Plains Indians along the way? Write about it on the back of this paper.

J332005 Clearly Social Studies

The Eastern Woodlands

The people of the Eastern Woodlands lived among vast forests and great lakes. Many hunted deer, birds, bear, and other woodland animals. They collected berries and nuts. Others fished in the rivers and picked wild rice beside the lakes. Some farmed crops such as corn, squash, and beans. The various tribes of the Woodlands Indians spoke about 68 different languages!

The two languages spoken most often were Iroquoian and Algonquian. These two languages divide the Woodlands Indians into two main groups—Iroquois and Algonquin. The Iroquois lived in longhouses covered with bark. The Algonquin lived in bark-covered cabins in winter and wigwams in summer. **Wigwams** were made from bent willow poles and covered with bark.

The Iroquois and the Algonquin fought over trade and land, yet both groups had something special in common. They lived in clans. A **clan** is a cluster of families who have the same ancestors. Each clan had its own special animal or plant to represent it—the Deer clan or the Potato clan. Each clan had its own responsibilities and legends. Clan members helped each other. Clan members from different tribes thought of themselves as family if they belonged to the same clan. The leaders of the clans were women—clan mothers. Women had lots of power! They determined who would use the land and how it was to be used.

Use words from above to complete the sentences.

1. Woodlands Indians lived among large _____ and _____ .

2. They often picked _____ _____, which grew beside the water.

3. Some tribes farmed _____ , _____, and _____ .

4. _____ and _____ were the two main languages.

5. Bark-covered Iroquois homes were called _____ .

6. The Algonquin wigwams were made from bent _____ _____ .

7. The leaders of the clans were called the _____ _____ .

8. The groups shared a lot yet they fought over _____ and _____ .

BONUS! Work with two other classmates to do this project. Make sure there is at least one girl in your group. Form a clan similar to a Woodland Indian clan. Choose a plant or animal name. Draw a picture of a clan banner. Write a short legend, or story, about how the plant (or animal) became important to you. List two responsibilities at school that your clan is in charge of.

Exploring North America

By studying early explorers and the many reasons for their explorations, the students will see how they began changing the way of life in North America.

Super Explorer

Help your students imagine what it must have been like to be an early explorer by reading some books such as the following:

- *Brendan the Navigator: A History Mystery of America* by Jean Fritz (Putnam, 1980)

- *The First Voyage Around the World* by Roger Coote (Bookwright Press, 1990)

- *I Sailed With Columbus* by Miriam Schlein (HarperCollins, 1991)

- *Pedro's Journal* by Pam Conrad (Caroline House, 1991)

- *Westward With Columbus* by John Dyson (Scholastic, 1991)

- *Where Do You Think You're Going, Christopher Columbus?* by Jean Fritz (Putnam, 1980)

Discuss what it must have felt like to be the captain of a ship sailing into the unknown. Ask the students what qualities a good explorer should have. Have the students list them on chart paper. Then write a classroom profile of a *super explorer*. As you read about explorers, have the students compare their super explorer with the real thing!

The Final Frontier

Tell your students that space is considered the "final frontier." Discuss why. Then place the students into small "crews." Tell the crews that they are convinced that life exists on another planet. Explain that each crew is to follow these directions:

1. Choose a captain.
2. List the responsibilities that each crew member is in charge of.
3. Decide which planet to explore.
4. Calculate how long your journey will take. (Assume that light-speed travel is standard.)
5. List the supplies and equipment you will need.
6. Draw the shuttle you will need to build to make your journey.
7. Plan a speech that persuades the president to fund your exploration.
8. Draw a map of your route.
9. Write three main journal entries—the first day of your journey, what you encounter when you explore your destination, and what happens the day you return to Earth.
10. Draw a picture of your crew.

Give the students plenty of time to work on this exciting project. Have each crew make a presentation to the rest of the class.

Shipbuilders

Share with the students that Christopher Columbus sailed on a *caravel*. This small, fast sailing ship was built by setting up the ribs before nailing on the outer planks of wood. Place the students in small groups of "shipbuilders." Have each group design and build a raft using the following materials:

Materials:
- craft sticks
- scissors
- string
- glue
- straws (for masts)
- sturdy white paper or tagboard (for sails)
- dishpan or tub of water

Directions:

1. Build a sailing ship or raft using craft sticks, glue, string, straws, and paper. Try to attach more than one sail. Use your imagination!
2. Test your ship's buoyancy. See how well it stays afloat. If it tips or sinks, rebuild your ship back in "dry dock."
3. Test your ship's speed. Place it on the water at one end of the dishpan or tub, blow on the sails, and time your ship to see long it takes to sail across the water.
4. Once your ship is seaworthy, challenge another group to a race!

Where Am I?

Transparency 2

Use Transparency 2, *World Map,* to make a copy of a world map for each student. Make a simple pattern of a sailboat and reproduce it so that each student has one. Have each student cut out the sailboat and glue it to the top of a large craft stick. Display Transparency 2 and play an explorer game by following these directions:

Each student is a world explorer. Think of an area on the transparency "to place yourself," but don't tell the explorers the location. Call out the degrees of latitude and longitude of the location. Say to the students: "Where Am I?" The explorers race to use the information to locate where in the world you are! When an explorer thinks he or she has found you, the explorer draws a red mark on the spot on his or her map and raises a craft stick. Award points to the first five explorers who locate you correctly! Challenge different students to take your place in deciding where to be.

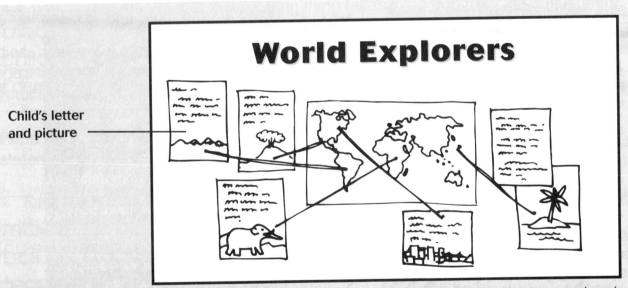

Child's letter and picture

Have each student imagine that he or she is an explorer who wishes to lead an expedition to somewhere in the world. Post a world map and review with the students the seven continents and major oceans. Give each student a copy of a world map by reproducing Transparency 2 on page 58. Have each student write the president of the United States a letter explaining the reasons for the exploration and a request for money to fund the trip. On the letter, have each student draw a picture of the area to be explored. Post each letter around the world map and use a length of yarn to connect it to the exploration site.

Finding Your Way

Christopher Columbus and other early explorers used a simple instrument called an astrolabe to help them navigate on the ocean. **Astrolabe** means "star finder." As they sailed north of the equator, they would measure the angle of the Pole Star (North Star), which was directly over the North Pole. This was the way explorers calculated their approximate latitude.

Follow the directions to make your own astrolabe.

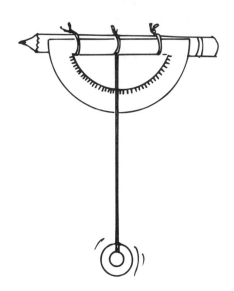

Materials:

- protractor
- string
- washer (or other weight)
- new, sharpened pencil
- scissors

Directions:

1. Cut a length of string about 15 inches long. Tie one end of the string to the middle of the straight side of the protractor. (The string should fall a little below the protractor.)

2. Tie the weight onto the other end of the string.

3. Lay the straight side of the protractor next to the pencil. Tie the two together with string.

How to Use Your Astrolabe:

1. Find the North Star. It is seen only in the northern part of the sky on a clear night. To help you, find the Big Dipper—the constellation that looks like a dipper with a long handle. The cup part of the dipper points to the North Star.

2. Point your astrolabe at the North Star. Aim with the point of your pencil.

3. The string will drop down and rest against one of the degree marks on the arc. Hold the string still. Read the number. This is your latitude number. Look at a map to check the latitude.

Teacher: Make copies of Transparency 2 on page 58 so that each student has a world map.

J332005 Clearly Social Studies

Name _____

Early Explorers

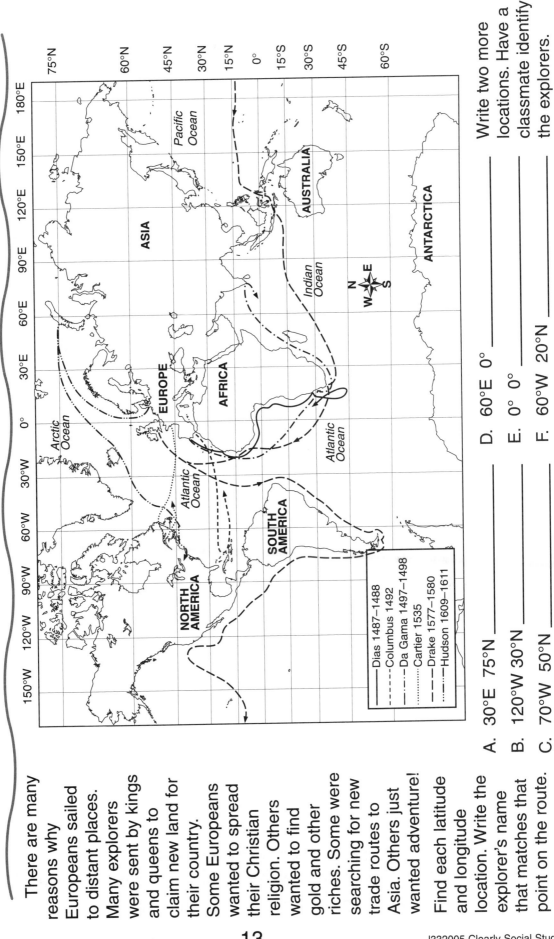

There are many reasons why Europeans sailed to distant places. Many explorers were sent by kings and queens to claim new land for their country. Some Europeans wanted to spread their Christian religion. Others wanted to find gold and other riches. Some were searching for new trade routes to Asia. Others just wanted adventure!

Find each latitude and longitude location. Write the explorer's name that matches that point on the route.

A. 30°E 75°N
B. 120°W 30°N
C. 70°W 50°N

D. 60°E 0°
E. 0° 0°
F. 60°W 20°N

Write two more locations. Have a classmate identify the explorers.

_____

_____

Map legend:
- Dias 1487–1488
- Columbus 1492
- Da Gama 1497–1498
- Cartier 1535
- Drake 1577–1580
- Hudson 1609–1611

Name _____

France and Spain Explore the Americas

Many French and Spanish explorers claimed land in the Americas for their countries. Use the map to answer the questions.

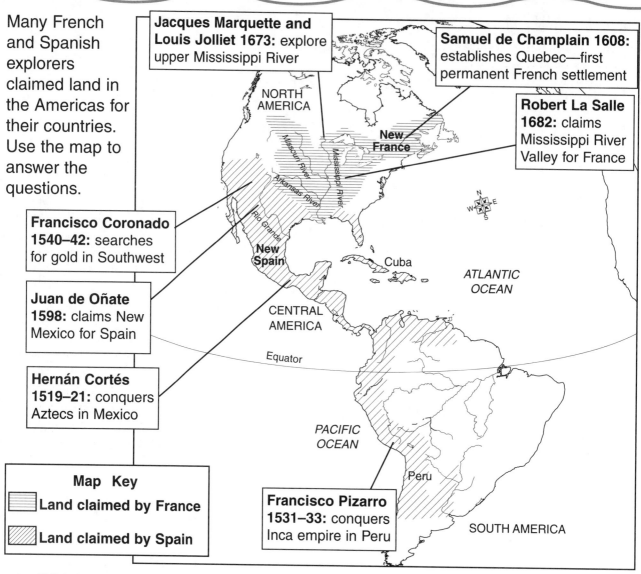

Jacques Marquette and Louis Jolliet 1673: explore upper Mississippi River

Samuel de Champlain 1608: establishes Quebec—first permanent French settlement

Robert La Salle 1682: claims Mississippi River Valley for France

Francisco Coronado 1540–42: searches for gold in Southwest

Juan de Oñate 1598: claims New Mexico for Spain

Hernán Cortés 1519–21: conquers Aztecs in Mexico

NORTH AMERICA

New France

Missouri River

Mississippi River

Arkansas River

Rio Grande

New Spain

Cuba

ATLANTIC OCEAN

CENTRAL AMERICA

Equator

PACIFIC OCEAN

Peru

SOUTH AMERICA

Map Key
Land claimed by France
Land claimed by Spain

Francisco Pizarro 1531–33: conquers Inca empire in Peru

1. Which main rivers did the French control? _____

_____

2. Which explorers helped to create the colony of New Spain? _____

_____

3. Who explored more land—the French or the Spanish? Support your answer.

_____

_____

4. On the back of this paper, write your answer to **one** of the following questions:

• Why do you think France and Spain wanted colonies in the Americas?

• Why do you think France and Spain didn't explore more of the West?

J332005 Clearly Social Studies

Name _____

The Changing Americas

Explorers brought about change in the Americas. Read about some of the effects these explorers had. Use the web map to answer the questions.

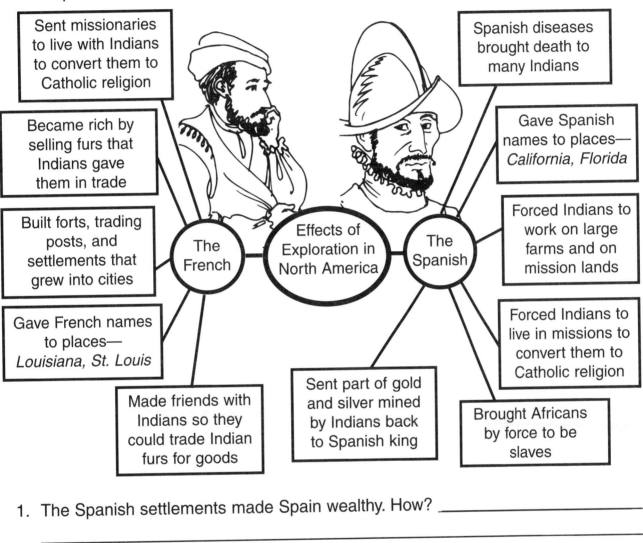

Sent missionaries to live with Indians to convert them to Catholic religion

Became rich by selling furs that Indians gave them in trade

Built forts, trading posts, and settlements that grew into cities

Gave French names to places— *Louisiana, St. Louis*

Made friends with Indians so they could trade Indian furs for goods

The French

Effects of Exploration in North America

The Spanish

Spanish diseases brought death to many Indians

Gave Spanish names to places— *California, Florida*

Forced Indians to work on large farms and on mission lands

Forced Indians to live in missions to convert them to Catholic religion

Sent part of gold and silver mined by Indians back to Spanish king

Brought Africans by force to be slaves

1. The Spanish settlements made Spain wealthy. How? _____
_____

2. The French missionaries seemed kinder to the Indians than the Spanish. How?
_____
_____

3. How did New France become rich because of the Indians? _____
_____

4. Why were French trading posts important in the future of North America?
_____

5. Which group of explorers do you think brought more negative effects to the Americas? Why do you think so? Write on the back of this paper.

SETTLING THE COLONIES

Help your students understand the hardships, courage, and adventure involved in settling America and making it grow.

Set the Scene

Prepare your students for their study of the lives of colonists by reading books such as the following:

- *American Kids in History: Colonial Days* by David C. King (Scholastic, 1998)

- *Charlie's House* by Clyde Robert Bulla (Crowell, 1983)

- *The Double Life of Pocahontas* by Jean Fritz (Putnam, 1983)

- *If You Lived in Williamsburg in Colonial Days* by Barbara Brenner (Scholastic, 2000)

- *The Sign of the Beaver* by Elizabeth George Speare (Houghton Mifflin, 1983)

After reading a few books, place the students in small groups to present a skit about part of one of the books you read. Let each group plan, write, practice, and present its skit for the rest of the class.

Colonial Trade

Transparency 3

Display Transparency 3, *Colonial Trade Routes*. Help the students understand how important trade was to the colonies by asking questions such as the following:

- *A merchant shipped slaves from Africa to the West Indies and sold them there for molasses. What did the New England colonies make with the molasses? Do you think this new product was more valuable than slaves? Why or why not?*

- *What was the difference between the goods traded from Great Britain and those from the colonies? Would this create conflict?*

Pomander Balls in Two Weeks

Tell your students that colonists made pomander balls to add fragrance in their houses and to carry with them when they called on people who were ill. (They thought the pomander's fragrance would keep them from getting sick.) Have each student make a pomander ball by following these directions:

Materials:
- newspaper
- wax paper
- small orange or lemon
- masking tape
- ribbon (or yarn)
- jar of whole cloves
- fork
- cinnamon, nutmeg, ginger, and other spices

Directions:

1. Cover your work space with newspaper.
2. Wrap a length of tape around the orange. Wrap another length of tape in the other direction so you divide the orange into quarters. The tape makes a path for the ribbon.
3. Poke shallow holes all around the orange using the fork. Do not poke holes through the tape.
4. Push a clove into each hole.
5. Remove the tape.
6. Sprinkle spices on a sheet of wax paper. Roll the orange in the mix. Wrap up the orange in wax paper and store it in a cool, dark place for two weeks. (It will shrink as it dries.) When the skin feels dry, the pomander is ready.
7. Unwrap the orange. Gently shake off any loose spices. Lay ribbon in paths left by the tape. Tie a double knot and bow at the top.
8. Slide another length of ribbon under the bow and make a loop. Hang the pomander ball in your room for a fragrant decoration!

The Quoits Game

Tell the students that *quoits* is a game that colonial children liked to play by tossing circles of rope, leather, or willow branches onto a stake. Assign each student a partner. Have each pair of students make a quoits game by following these directions:

Materials:

- clothesline
- masking tape
- ruler
- scissors
- red and black markers
- 20-inch wooden dowel

Making the game:

1. Measure and cut four 15-inch pieces of rope.
2. Loop each piece into a circle and join the ends by wrapping masking tape several times around where the ends meet to make a quoit.
3. Color the masking tape on the quoits to make two red quoits and two black ones.

Playing the game:

1. Push the dowel into the ground to make a hob, or peg. Walk about 10–15 feet away from the hob and lay a length of clothesline down to mark a tossing line where each player stands.
2. Angle the hob so it points toward the tossing line. Practice tossing a quoit onto the hob.
3. The first player tries to toss either the red or the black quoits onto the hob. The second player then tosses his or her two quoits.
4. If a quoit encircles the hob (a ringer), the player gets 5 points. But if the player's opponent gets a ringer on top of the first ringer, no points are scored!
5. If there are no ringers, whoever has the quoit closest to the hob, gets 2 points.
6. The first player to score 20 points wins!

We're Settling Down

Group pictures

Place your students in small groups. Have the students imagine that they are colonists trying to find a place in the new world to build a colony. Have each group first draw a picture of an ideal area. Remind the students that colonists needed a good source of water, good farm land, hills or cliffs for protection, resources for food and for building materials, and ways to travel. Then have each group draw what its colony looks like using the same landscape they drew in the first picture. Tell the groups to name their settlements. Let each group explain its drawings to the rest of the class. Post the drawings side by side.

Name _____

Colonial Products

Trading goods helped the colonies grow and prosper. Follow the directions to finish this product map. (Use a U.S.A. map to help you identify the colonies.)

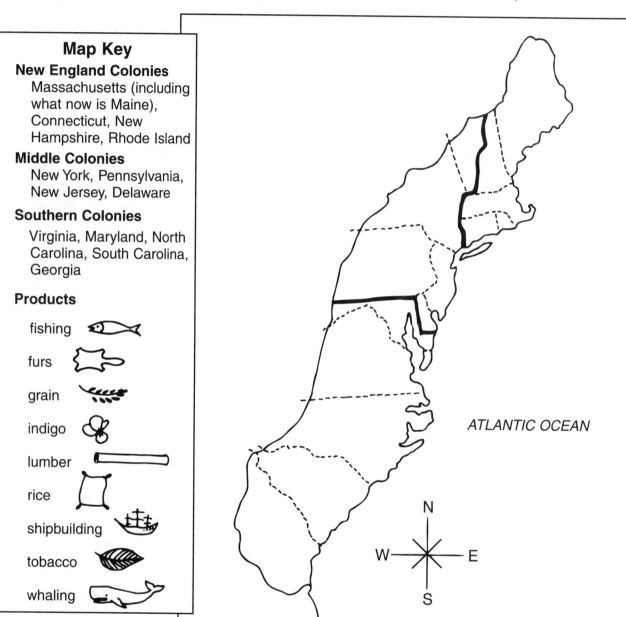

Map Key

New England Colonies
Massachusetts (including what now is Maine), Connecticut, New Hampshire, Rhode Island

Middle Colonies
New York, Pennsylvania, New Jersey, Delaware

Southern Colonies
Virginia, Maryland, North Carolina, South Carolina, Georgia

Products

fishing

furs

grain

indigo

lumber

rice

shipbuilding

tobacco

whaling

ATLANTIC OCEAN

1. Draw the product symbols on or near the matching colonies: New England Colonies—whaling, fishing, shipbuilding, furs, lumber. Middle Colonies—furs, grain, lumber. Southern Colonies—grain, tobacco, fishing, indigo, lumber, rice.

2. Lightly color the New England Colonies orange, the Middle Colonies purple, and the Southern Colonies yellow.

3. Write five map questions. Exchange questions with a classmate.

The Jamestown River

In 1607, about 100 men and boys landed in Virginia. They were soldiers, convicts, and adventurers. Merchants from England had paid their way. In return, they were to give the merchants a share of any gold they found or crops they grew. The plan was to get rich quick and return to England.

They built a settlement by the James River and called it Jamestown in honor of England's king. They built upriver so they would be protected from an ocean attack. If the Indians came at them by land, they could escape out to sea on the river. They carried goods up and down the river. The river provided fish, wildlife, and fresh water. What a perfect place, or so they thought!

At high tide, the ocean spilled into the river and contaminated the water. The river made the land a swamp. These men weren't farmers and had no clue how to grow crops on swamp land. Mosquitoes lived in the swamps and carried malaria, typhoid fever, and other deadly diseases. After six months, more than half of the men had died!

The plan had failed. The men weren't used to such hard work. They fought and argued. Captain John Smith took charge. He ruled that those who didn't work, didn't eat. He forced the men to build, to hunt, and to farm. He set up trade with the Powhatan for food. Smith was very strict. Without his leadership, Jamestown would not have survived.

One way to help you remember what you read is to write a sentence outline. On another piece of paper, write and complete this outline of the above information.

I. There were reasons why Jamestown was to be built.
   A. The colonists were to give the merchants _____
   B. The colonists had a plan to _____

II. There were advantages in settling by a river.
   A. The river would protect the men _____
   B. They could escape _____
   C. They carried their goods _____
   D. The river gave them _____

III. There were disadvantages in settling by a river.
   A. At high tide, _____
   B. The water made the land _____
   C. Mosquitoes _____

IV. Captain John Smith helped Jamestown succeed.
   A. He ruled that _____
   B. He forced the men _____
   C. He traded with _____

J332005 Clearly Social Studies

Servants and Slaves

To help its Virginia colonies grow, England decided to send workers instead of adventurers to America. English merchants paid the ocean passage for anyone willing to work for them as an **indentured servant** for up to seven years. After completing the work, an indentured servant was given freedom, clothing, and land. Many people who were unhappy with life in England chose this way to come to America. England even promised to give land to people for every indentured servant they brought to America! These new settlers soon owned hundreds of acres of large farms called **plantations**.

Many plantation owners grew tobacco as a **cash crop**—a crop to sell and not to use for themselves. They grew rich and greedy for more workers. But as life in England improved, fewer people wanted to come to America. Many of the indentured servants already in America refused to work the backbreaking hours on the plantations. They chose to go to other colonies to work off their debts. So the colonists forced Indians from their own land to work as slaves. But many of these Indians died from exhaustion and disease, and others escaped to freedom. Indians had rights and choices when they lived on land away from the "white people." So colonists bought African slaves. These men, women, and children had no rights, no choices. They were property—sold and auctioned off. They worked *all* their lives as slaves and never shared in the riches that they helped to create.

Use the information above to help you complete this chart. Then on the back of this paper, answer: *Which of the three types of workers had the "best" life? Why?*

	Length of Time Required to Work for Someone	Rights They Had	Choices They Were Given	Land They Could Own	When They Could Gain Freedom
Indentured Servant					
American Indian					
African Slave					

J332005 Clearly Social Studies

New England Life

The New England colonies were started by the Puritans. Their leader was John Winthrop. They left England so that they could practice their Christian beliefs away from the grand Church of England. They believed in hard work and simple living. They believed all other religions were wrong. Some Puritans voiced different beliefs and were more tolerant toward Indians. Two of these people, Roger Williams and Anne Hutchinson, even started their own colonies.

Study the chart. Use the information to answer the questions.

Life in the New England Colonies						
Resources	Climate	Land/Water	Government	Religion	Family Life	Child's Life
coastal waters filled with fish; dense forests with lumber and wildlife	short summers; cold, long winters; growing season lasting four to five months	harbors, bays, lakes, ponds, rivers; thin layer of rocky soil; rounded mountains	not a democracy; only male church members could vote and govern; colonists led by Bible teachings	simple Christian beliefs; Puritans thought theirs was the *only* religion; ministers controlled	very large families; lived and worked closely together; did chores, studied, and ate in a "keeping room"	taught to read Bible; learned religion; some boys learned a trade; had toys until age 7; did many chores

1. Why was farming difficult in the New England colonies? _____

_____

2. The "keeping room" was a large downstairs room where a fireplace was kept going all the time. In winter, families slept there. How else did families use the "keeping room"? _____

_____

3. Why was teaching children to read important to the Puritans?_____

_____

4. Did Puritans believe in democracy?_____

_____

5. How do you think people like Anne Hutchinson were important to the development of New England? Write your answer on the back of this paper.

J332005 Clearly Social Studies

The Middle Colonies

The geography of the Middle Colonies made the area a good place to settle. The coast provided land for the colonists to build major ports and trade centers. The river valleys provided the farmers with fertile soil for growing crops and the fur trappers with a wealth of wildlife. These rivers also provided a way for the colonists to transport their goods between the cities.

Use this map to answer the questions.

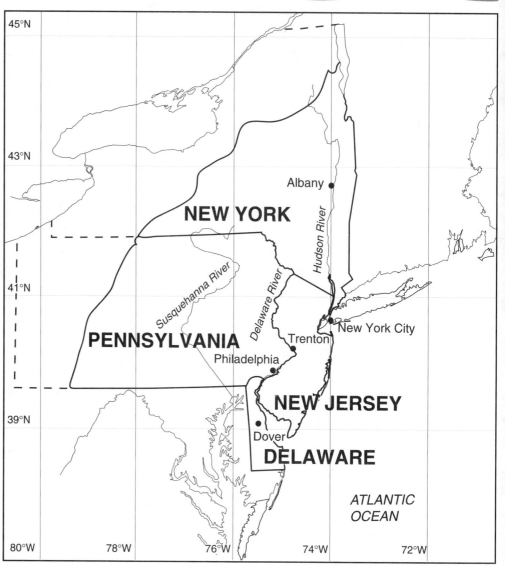

1. Which latitude line is closest to Albany, New York? _____

2. On which longitude line is the city of New York? _____

3. Along which longitude line does the Hudson River run? _____

4. Which city is closest to where 39°N latitude and 76°W longitude intersect?

   _____

5. In which state do 43°N latitude and 74°W longitude intersect? _____

6. Which river is closest to where 41°N latitude and 76°W longitude intersect?

   _____

7. On which latitude line does the Delaware River cross? _____

Write two more map questions. Use the back of this paper. Exchange with a friend.

Pilgrims and Quakers

Read about two men who each led a different group of people to America.

I am William Bradford. I and my followers sailed to America so we could practice our Christian beliefs freely. England had said everyone must belong to the Church of England. It was much too grand for us. We worship simply. We were also afraid that we'd be put in prison. We call ourselves "Pilgrims" because we are people on a holy journey. We've settled near Cape Cod, far from Virginia, where we had planned to go. Some of our people didn't like this choice, so we wrote an agreement that said we all had to follow what our leaders decided. We wrote this on our ship, the *Mayflower*, so we called it the Mayflower Compact. We govern ourselves!

We lived on the *Mayflower* while we cleared the land and built Plymouth Colony. But our first winter was freezing cold! Sadly, we buried more than half of our people. In spring, an Indian named Squanto taught us how to plant corn and where to hunt. We have made peace with the Wampanoag. We even held a three-day harvest feast with the Indians to thank God for our blessings.

I am William Penn. I sailed to America with a group of people who wanted to practice Christian beliefs freely. Because I didn't want to belong to the Church of England and practiced Christianity another way, I was put in prison many times. My friends feared prison, too. We are called "Quakers" because we quake at the word of God. We believe everyone is equal in God's eyes. We have formed a colony called Pennsylvania. I call our colony a "Holy Experiment." It was land given to me by the king of England, who owed my father a large debt. We invite all who believe in God to come live here and practice their religion freely.

We have built a beautiful capital city called Philadelphia, meaning "brotherly love." I have written a plan on how to govern ourselves. This plan promises religious freedom for all who believe in God and gives the people a voice in our government. Even women have more freedom and power here than in other colonies. We have made peace with the Delaware and respect their rights.

With a partner, answer these questions. Write on the back of this paper.

1. Most of the colonists on the Mayflower were hired workers. Many of the workers wanted to settle in the warmer climate of Virginia. What might have happened to the Pilgrims and Plymouth if these workers didn't sign the Mayflower Compact?

2. William Bradford and William Penn were two great colonial leaders. How were their leadership, lives, and beliefs similar? What was different about the men?

J332005 Clearly Social Studies

SHAPING THE COLONIES

Your students will better appreciate their world as they learn about the events and the people who helped shape America in a time of conflict and growth.

A Tug of Land

Explain to the students that many groups were struggling to control the land in America—a nation of Indians (such as the Huron), French trappers, and British colonists. Place

your students in three groups. Assign each group a role to play: the Indians, who are trying to maintain their ownership of the land; the French, who want to claim the land for hunting and trapping; and the British colonists, who want to create more farms and settlements for the expanding population. The Indians, the French

trappers, and the British settlers cannot share the land, and Great Britain and France are close to starting a war over it. Have each group plan and write an argument that gives reasons why the land should belong to its members. Give the groups time to practice their

arguments before they present them to the rest of the class. Encourage the students to play their parts with enthusiasm and drama. Tell them that they might even dress up for their roles! If you want to add excitement, invite another class to listen to the arguments. Reward the most convincing argument!

Web Mapping

Transparency 4

Display Transparency 4, *Web Mapping*. With the students, create a web map that shows how Great Britain tried to control the colonies through taxes and duties. In the center of the web, write *How Britain Tried to Control the Colonies*. On each branch, write one of the ways Great Britain tried to do this: *Sugar Act* (increased the number of customs agents to catch smugglers of molasses into the colonies), *Stamp Act* (extra charge on newspapers and other written items that required a government stamp on them to show a tax was paid), *Townshend Acts* (duties colonists paid on paper, lead, tea, and painters' colors; named for Charles Townshend, who was in charge of handling the money), and *soldiers* (reinforcements to keep order and control).

Ask the students why they think Great Britain tried to control the colonists with taxes and duties (to help finance English merchants and trading companies and to help build up the English treasury after the French and Indian War).

Reproduce Transparency 4 so that each student has a web map. Talk with the students about what it means to control a country, a class, or a person. Then have them imagine that they are each teacher for the day. Have each student write his or her name in the center of the web and on each branch write one way he or she would "control" the class as teacher. Give the students time to think and write before letting each of them share his or her web.

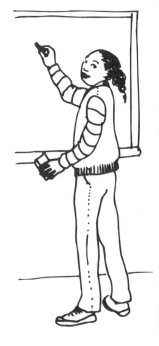

To Be Free or Not to Be Free!

Place the students into three groups—the British Parliament; the loyal colonists, who wanted to stay protected by Great Britain; and the patriots, who wanted the colonies to be independent. Tell the students that they are going to participate in a dramatization of how the two groups of colonists might have posed their arguments before Parliament and what the British government's response might have been to both groups. If possible, have the students dress the parts. Set up each member of Parliament on a chair in front of the classroom. Have each group argue why it should or shouldn't be a part of Great Britain. Let the members of Parliament respond.

After the skit, talk with the students about how each group felt as it participated in the drama. Discuss how hard it was for each group to change its views.

Tall Tale Fun

Share with the students that many of the tall tales in American literature are about frontier men and women called "pathfinders," who helped settle land west of the Appalachian Mountains. Tell the students that the most famous of these pioneers was Daniel Boone. Remind the students that tall tales greatly exaggerate the adventures of these people. Have each student choose an area in the United States—Rocky Mountains, Great Plains, etc.— and write a tall tale about himself or herself exploring that region. Review that tall tales often explain how mountains, deserts, or other landforms were created. (e.g., Paul Bunyan dug the Great Lakes because his blue ox, Babe, was thirsty!) Encourage the students to have fun with their stories and to illustrate them!

Student Advertisements

Talk with your students about how some colonists who wanted to be free from British control wrote newspaper stories trying to win support in the colonies for their side. Post the word *propaganda* on a bulletin board. Discuss how propaganda tells only one side of a story in order to convince someone to think a certain way or to buy a certain item. Review with the students how colonial propaganda stirred up anger and resentment toward the British. Explain that propaganda has been used throughout history and is used today. Place the students in small groups. Give each group a stack of newspapers, scissors, construction paper, markers, and glue. Tell the groups to search through the newspapers to find "propaganda" ads that try to convince people to buy a product based on its "wonderful" qualities. Tell the students to each find two ads, cut them out, and glue each one to a sheet of construction paper. Have the students write at the bottom of their ads how the authors are trying to sway the reader. Let the students discuss their ads before pinning them on the bulletin board.

As a follow-up activity, have each student design an ad to either convince the colonists to be independent of British rule or to remain loyal British citizens. Post these ads next to the displayed advertisements.

The French and Indian War

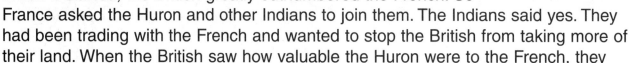

By 1754, the Indians, the French, and the British were claiming the same land in the Ohio River Valley. French hunters and trappers wanted the land as a source of fish and wildlife. They had been shipping animal furs and fish from the wilderness to their country and making large profits. The British wanted the land for farms and settlements for colonists. When the British began to move west, the French built forts to stop them.

The British governor of Virginia sent George Washington with a group of soldiers to force the French to leave. A war began. When it started, the British greatly outnumbered the French. So France asked the Huron and other Indians to join them. The Indians said yes. They had been trading with the French and wanted to stop the British from taking more of their land. When the British saw how valuable the Huron were to the French, they

asked the Iroquois to join them. (The Iroquois and the Huron were enemies.) The British promised not to settle on Iroquois lands. The Iroquois agreed to fight. France kept winning battles until Great Britain sent better officers and more troops to America. The French were finally defeated.

The war had many effects. Great Britain gained Florida, much of Canada, and most of New France. It also had spent a lot of money and was heavily in debt. The Iroquois and other Indians realized that they didn't have much power over the colonists, and the colonists gained confidence in themselves.

Answer the questions using complete sentences.

1. Why did France want colonies in America? _____

_____

2. Why did France build forts in the Ohio River Valley? _____

_____

3. How did the British respond to the new forts?

_____

4. Why do you think the French asked the Huron to join them? _____

_____

5. Why do you think this war is called the "French and Indian War"? _____

_____

6. How did the war affect America? Write your answer on the back of this paper.

British Taxes

By helping the colonists win the French and Indian War, Great Britain had drained its treasury. Britain decided to raise money from the colonists by taxing them. Read what happened. Then answer the questions on the back of this paper.

In 1764, Britain made it harder to smuggle molasses so that Colonial merchants were forced to pay a British tax on molasses. This was called the **Sugar Act**. Colonial leaders protested. They wanted Parliament, the British government, to do away with this act. They said Britain didn't have the right to tax people who weren't represented by members of Parliament. Parliament lowered the tax but didn't repeal it.

The next year, Parliament said that colonists had to pay a tax each time they bought newspapers or other legal documents. These items had to have a government stamp on them to show that the tax was paid. The colonists protested this **Stamp Act**. Angry colonists spoke out. Men formed the Sons of Liberty. Women formed the Daughters of Liberty. Some of the "sons of liberty" attacked the stamp-tax agents and forced them to quit their jobs. Parliament repealed the Stamp Act!

Two years later, Parliament set up a tax on any lead, paper, paint, glass, and tea that came from Britain. These taxes were called the **Townshend Acts** after Charles Townshend, the British treasurer. The colonists agreed to boycott, or refuse to buy, any goods imported from Britain. The Daughters of Liberty spun thread so colonists wouldn't buy cloth from Britain. Colonists pressured the merchants not to buy British goods. The boycott worked! Parliament repealed all the taxes, except the tax on tea.

1. Why were the colonial merchants forced to pay a tax on molasses?

2. What did Parliament do when the colonists protested the Sugar Act?

3. What was the effect of the Stamp Act on colonial men and women?

4. How did the colonists decide to protest the Townshend Acts?

5. Why did Parliament repeal the Townshend Acts (except the tax on tea)?

6. Why do you think the British kept their tax on tea?

7. With each tax, the colonists forced Parliament to repeal or reduce its taxes. Why do you think the colonists were so effective? Write on the back of this paper.

J332005 Clearly Social Studies

"The Boston Tea Party" Play

CHARACTERS: Abigail Adams   John Adams   Paul Revere   King George III
(2) Boston colonists   Governor Hutchinson   Messenger   George Robert Twelves Hewes

Scene One: 1773 in King George III's Palace in Great Britain

KING GEORGE III: Colonists give me a headache! We fight the French for them in war. We send them soldiers and supplies. Our treasuries are empty. Now we need money and they cry, "NO taxes!" Well, we shall see about this. *(calls out)* Messenger!

(Enter Messenger.)

MESSENGER: Yes, Sire?

KING GEORGE III: Send this message to our American colonies at once. England will keep its tax on tea! Expect our first shipment of English tea in Boston around November.

MESSENGER: Forgive my impudence, Sire, but won't the colonists resist? They hate our tea tax.

KING GEORGE III: They wouldn't dare resist! We'll sell our tea at such a low price, they can't refuse to buy it. We'll get our tax money yet.

Scene Two: Boston in November 1773; Home of John and Abigail Adams

ABIGAIL ADAMS: My, dear, the tea . . . is arrived. . . . I hope opposition has been made to the landing of it. . . . The flame is kindled and like lightning it catches from Soul to Soul.

JOHN ADAMS: I feel the flame, too, my dear . . . we must preserve our liberty.

Scene Three: Three Weeks Later in Boston *(Paul Revere, George Hewes, and Boston colonists crowd around a posted sign.)*

GEORGE HEWES: *(laughing)* Well, we've shown the British. A pox on their tea tax! We've crowded the docks for weeks. No one can unload the tea.

PAUL REVERE: Look what's posted here . . . *The tea-ships being arrived, every inhabitant who wishes to preserve the Liberty of America is desired to meet at the State-House, precisely at TEN o'clock to advise what is to be done on this alarming crisis.* Well, I'm for liberty. Anyone else?

COLONISTS: We are! To the state-house in the morning!

 J332005 Clearly Social Studies

Scene Four: Nighttime in December 1773, Boston Harbor	
PAUL REVERE:	Silence, men. The time is right. The tide is low. Quickly rub your faces with this charcoal. Here, some use this soot and burnt cork. Put on your Mohawk clothes. Hah! What disguises!
GEORGE HEWES:	*(whispers)* Ready, men? Be silent. Let's sneak onto the ships. *(Men go onto ships.)* Cut and slit open the tea chests. Use your hatchets. Dump the tea overboard into the harbor.
COLONISTS:	*(whispers)* But there's more than 300 chests, Hewes! *(Three hours later)*
GEORGE HEWES:	The tea is laying on the water like sand dunes.
PAUL REVERE:	*(laughing)* Yes, like piles of hay! Boston Harbor is a teapot!
COLONISTS:	Hewes, someone has broken a padlock.
GEORGE HEWES:	Ack . . . we'll have to replace it tomorrow. But no more damage, men. Now . . . let's get to sweeping the decks clean. Be quick!

Scene Five: Days Later in Boston	
GOVERNOR:	Ooh . . . we still don't know who did this horrible deed! Such clever disguises! King George is furious. He demands that Boston be punished. All of us! He's closing our port. How will we get food and supplies? We must pay for the spoiled tea or starve.
COLONISTS:	The king's ordered us to feed the British soldiers, too. And house them. . . . These acts are intolerable!

Scene Six: Later in Boston at Home of John and Abigail Adams	
ABIGAIL ADAMS:	Boston is holding to liberty, my dear. The Committees of Correspondence have been secretly sending us food and money. They unite us. They tell us not to pay for an ounce of tea.
JOHN ADAMS:	*(writing in a journal while speaking)* These committees are a great political engine. They move us closer to independence.
ABIGAIL ADAMS:	What is that you're writing in your journal today?
JOHN ADAMS:	Ah, my account of the Boston Tea Party. . . . *The people should never rise without doing something to be remembered—something notable and striking. This destruction of the tea is so bold, so daring . . .*
ABIGAIL ADAMS:	We're in a new time in history, John.
JOHN ADAMS:	Yes, my dear Abigail, I believe that we are. *(The End)*

Brave Riders in the Night

Read the excerpted poem about Paul Revere and the poem about Sybil Ludington. On the back of this paper, write a paragraph describing how these two people were alike and different. Work in a group to illustrate one of the poems and read it aloud.

Paul Revere's Ride
by Henry Wadsworth Longfellow
(April 18, 1775)

Listen, my children, and you shall hear
Of the midnight ride of Paul Revere,
On the eighteenth of April, in seventy-five;
Hardly a man is now alive
Who remembers that famous day and year.
He said to his friend, "If the British march
By land or sea from the town tonight,
Hang a lantern aloft in the belfry arch
Of the North Church tower as a signal light,—
One, if by land, and two, if by sea;
And I on the opposite shore will be,
Ready to ride and spread the alarm
Through every Middlesex village and farm,
For the country folk to be up and to arm."

. . .

Meanwhile, impatient to mount and ride,
Booted and spurred, with a heavy stride
On the opposite shore walked Paul Revere.
Now he patted his horse's side,
Now gazed at the landscape far and near,
Then, impetuous, stamped the earth,
And turned and tightened his saddle-girth;

. . .

So through the night rode Paul Revere;
And so through the night went his cry of alarm
To every Middlesex village and farm,—
A cry of defiance and not of fear,
A voice in the darkness, a knock at the door,
And a word that shall echo forevermore!
For, borne on the night-wind of the Past,
Through all our history, to the last,
In the hour of darkness and peril and need,
The people will waken and listen to hear
The hurrying hoof-beats of that steed,
And the midnight message of Paul Revere.

Sybil Ludington's Ride
by Marsha Elyn Wright
(April 26, 1777)

Listen, my friends, and you will hear
Of Sybil Ludington's ride through forty miles of frontier,
On the twenty-sixth of April, in seventy-seven;
Most of the people are now up in Heaven
Who remember that famous night and year.
She said to her father who commanded the men,
"I'll carry a warning and spread the word,
That the British are burning city and glen!
I'll muster up men. My call will be heard,—
I'll rouse women and children to bundle up all,
To set free the livestock from their stall.
I'll ride Star this night to spread the alarm
On deep-rutted roads from farm to farm,
For the militia men to get up and to arm."

Sybil mounted young Star in the cold, wet night,
She patted and coaxed him to lessen his fright.
Rain wet her trousers; it soaked through her shawl;
It splashed on her face and blinded her sight.
She rode to each farmhouse and shouted her call,
"Rouse! Rouse! To arms! Quick open your shutter!"
"What's the alarm?" the farmers did mutter.

Sixteen-year-old Sybil on sure-footed Star
Pointed to burning Danbury to give her reply,
"The Redcoats are marching this way by and by!"
She repeated her message to farms near and far.
Through New York's woods she galloped all night
For America, for freedom, for a colonist's right!
Some thieves surprised her; chased after her steed.
She barely escaped them—a courageous deed.
Sybil galloped down Ludington Lane in a whirl,
Where her father awaited his midnight traveler,
"My work is done," cried the young soldier girl.
"I'm proud to report this to you, Father, sir!"

J332005 Clearly Social Studies

Brave People in the Revolutionary War

Many brave people helped America fight for independence. Read about some of them. After each paragraph, write a question that you would like to ask that person if he or she were alive today. On the back of this paper, write what you admire about one of the people. Write why you think he or she was important to America's history.

Mary Hays cooked and washed for soldiers. Her husband loaded and fired cannons. During a battle, when her husband became wounded, she took his place! Soldiers called her "Molly Pitcher" because she carried pitchers of water to thirsty soldiers.

Mercy Otis Warren wrote humorous plays about the British. Patriots often met in her home. She encouraged women to give up buying tea and other British goods so they'd stop paying British taxes. Later, she wrote books about the American Revolution.

1. _____

_____

2. _____

_____

Patrick Henry was a powerful speaker. His nickname was "the Son of Thunder." He helped convince colonists to fight for freedom from Britain. In his greatest speech he said, ". . . give me liberty or give me death!" This speech was printed and read by many colonists who were stirred to action.

Thomas Paine wrote a pamphlet called *Common Sense*. He said a small island like Britain shouldn't rule a large continent like America. "A government of our own is our natural right," he wrote. Over 500,000 copies were sold in the colonies. His words convinced many colonists to fight for freedom.

3. _____

_____

4. _____

_____

Phillis Wheatley was kidnapped from Africa at eight years old to become a slave in America. Her owners taught her to read and write English. Later, she published poetry that pleaded with colonists to free their slaves. "In every human . . . God has implanted . . . (a) love of freedom. . . ." She even wrote a poem for General George Washington and visited him at his headquarters.

5. _____

J332005 Clearly Social Studies

Effects of the War

Read about how the American Revolution affected different people living in America. Then complete the chart below using the information from your reading.

Before the war, colonial women tended the gardens and made the clothes. They cared for the house and the children. When their husbands went to war, the women took over the men's jobs. They told the farm workers what to do. They ran flour mills and shops. They paid bills and managed the money. Women's roles really changed!

Before the war, many Indians lived on their own land. They often set up treaties with colonists to protect one another. After the war, the American government wanted to punish the Iroquois who fought with the British. The government burned their villages and set fire to their crops. It set up a treaty that gave America all Iroquois land west of New York and crowded the Indians into a small area. Many Iroquois moved to Canada.

Before the war, most African Americans were slaves. When the war started, Britain promised any enslaved man his freedom if he joined the British army. The colonial army promised freedom, too. After the war, about 14,000 freed African Americans left America. Some found jobs in Canada and England. Some returned to Africa.

About one out of three colonists didn't want to be free from England. These Loyalists fought against the Patriots, who wanted independence. They lived side by side with the Patriots. After the war, most Loyalists were treated badly. Congress wanted to take away their homes and property. About 80,000 Loyalists left America. The American government paid them nothing for their property.

Effects of the American Revolution		
	Before the War	During and After the War
Loyalists		
Colonial Women		
African American volunteers		
Indians who aided British		

Name _____

A Daring Declaration

After the start of the American Revolution in 1775, the Second Continental Congress agreed to send King George an offering of peace. They sent the "Olive Branch Petition." It stated that America was loyal to Britain and urged the king to end the Intolerable Acts and stop the fighting. The king refused to read it! He thought the Congress was illegal. In anger, he said he would "bring the traitors to justice."

The king's anger shocked the colonists. The fighting intensified. A year later, the Congress decided to make a declaration of independence. Thomas Jefferson was asked to write it. The first draft took Jefferson just two days! After Benjamin Franklin and John Adams made a few changes, they showed it to Congress.

The Declaration was made up of three main parts. The first part stated the "rights of all men." The second part had a list of strong complaints against King George. The third part was the actual declaration of independence of the states from Britain. After days of rewriting and arguing over Jefferson's words, the Declaration of Independence was approved on July 4, 1776. As each man signed his name, he knew he would be thought of as a traitor to England. British soldiers could arrest any of them. Benjamin Franklin said, "We must all hang together, or we shall all hang separately."

Write **agree** if you agree with each statement. Write **disagree** if you don't. Write why.

1. The Second Continental Congress wanted an end to the war. _____
   Why? _____

2. King George was right to refuse the Olive Branch Petition. _____
   Why? _____

3. Jefferson was important to the Second Continental Congress. _____
   Why? _____

4. When the men signed the Declaration, they had nothing to fear. _____
   Why? _____

5. Women should have helped to write the Declaration. _____ Why?

_____

Words of Declaration

One of the world's most important documents is the Declaration of Independence. Read the excerpts below. Use the **boldface** words to complete the word puzzle.

> *When in the **course** of human events, it becomes necessary for one people to **dissolve** the political bands which have connected them with another, . . . they should declare the causes which **impel** them to the **separation**.*
>
> *We hold these truths to be **self-evident**, that all men are created equal, that they are **endowed** by their Creator with certain **unalienable** Rights, that among these are Life, Liberty, and the **pursuit** of Happiness. . . .*
>
> *That whenever any Form of Government becomes **destructive** of these ends, it is the Right of the People to alter or to **abolish** it. . . .*

Across

4 provided
7 push
8 path or direction
9 get rid of
10 division

Down

1 destroying
2 cannot be taken away
3 seeking
5 break up
6 clear; obvious

Work with a partner. Read the following and answer the question together. Present your ideas to the rest of the class. *The Declaration said that "all men are created equal," yet women couldn't own property or vote. Native Americans didn't have the same rights as colonists. African Americans were slaves. What do you think Congress meant by "all men are created equal"? What does* <u>equality</u> *really mean?*

Steps toward a New Government

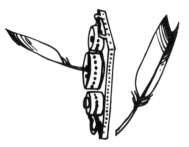

1781	1787	1787	1791
Articles of Confederation	*Northwest Ordinance*	*United States Constitution*	*Bill of Rights*
Set up first central government. Said each state could make its own laws, collect taxes, and print money. Some states didn't accept money from other states. Women couldn't vote or hold office. Congress didn't have power to settle disputes between states. States became more powerful than nation as a whole.	Provided government for Northwest Territory (land north of Ohio River, west of Pennsylvania, and east of Mississippi River). Set out rules for sections of territory to become states. Established rights of citizens. Recognized Native Americans' rights to own land and to be treated fairly. Outlawed slavery in the territory.	Set up three branches—legislative, executive, and judicial. Legislative branch made laws for America and collected taxes. Executive branch was headed by the president and was responsible for enforcing laws. Judicial branch decided meaning of laws. It was made up of Supreme Court judges.	Was first 10 amendments added to Constitution. (Amendments are changes in or additions to original Constitution.) Protected people's individual rights. Described basic rights of people in America. Guaranteed government cannot take away these rights.

Study the time line. Then answer the questions below. Write on the back of this paper.

1. After the Constitution was signed, how long did it take before the Bill of Rights was added?

2. Why did the states have so much power under the Articles of Confederation?

3. What are two good things the Northwest Ordinance did?

4. According to the Constitution, what are the three government branches and what do they do?

5. Why do you think the Bill of Rights was added to the Constitution?

J332005 Clearly Social Studies

Name _____

A Frontier Hero

In the 1700's, pioneers traveled into the West to find new places to live. The trails they followed began as Native American paths. Later, trailblazers marked the trails in better ways and opened up new trails to follow. One famous trailblazer was Daniel Boone. People made up exaggerated adventures about him called "tall tales."

Read the biography (left) and the tall tale about Boone. Then follow the directions.

Daniel Boone was born in 1734 in Pennsylvania. After his Quaker family moved to the North Carolina frontier, Boone learned how to hunt and shoot. He helped his family by trapping animals and selling their skins and furs.

When he was 22, he married Rebecca Bryan. With the hope for a better life, he led pioneers to the rich forests of Kentucky. The pioneers built a fort called Boonesborough. He returned to North Carolina to get his family and others. Boone led them to Kentucky along a new trail he had opened called the Wilderness Road. It became a main route to the west.

At 43, Boone was captured and adopted by the Shawnee. Later, he escaped to warn Boonesborough of an Indian attack and saved the fort. He died in 1820.

Daniel Boone was born in 1734 with adventure in his blood! While living on the North Carolina frontier with his Quaker family, Boone learned to shoot and hunt. He could shoot a beaver that was five miles away while blindfolded and backwards! Once on a hunting trip, Boone faced a buffalo stampede. He stood tall and aimed his rifle at the lead animal. With one shot, he knocked that buffalo to the ground! Boone sheltered his body behind the dead animal as the rest of the herd roared past. He didn't get one scratch!

Once he was captured by the Shawnee. But Boone just grinned so big at the chief that the sun bounced off of his teeth and lit up the forest like it was on fire. That Shawnee chief untied Boone and adopted him as a son!

1. Draw a picture for both the biography and the tall tale. Label each picture.

2. <u>Underline</u> the exaggerated details about Boone in the tall tale.

3. Write on the back of this paper how a biography is different from a tall tale.

4. Highlight the facts in the tall tale that match those in the biography.

5. On another sheet of paper, write a tall tale about Boone. Exaggerate an adventure he had while opening up the Wilderness Road. Illustrate it.

Name _____

The Lewis and Clark Expedition

President Thomas Jefferson wanted to learn about America's unexplored land. He asked his assistant Meriwether Lewis to lead an expedition to the Pacific Ocean. Lewis invited his friend William Clark to help lead. Their aim was to find a safe, direct river route to the Pacific Ocean. Jefferson also wanted them to write down all that they saw—the animals, the plants, and the people. Lewis and Clark chose soldiers, trappers, and frontiersmen for their journey. The men called themselves the "Corps of Discovery." A **corps** (kor) is a group working together for the same reason.

The corps left in boats from St. Louis in May 1804. They spent their first winter in a Mandan village, where they hired Toussaint Charbonneau (too SAHN SHAHR buh noh) and his 15-year-old Shoshone wife, Sacagawea (sah kah jah WEE uh), to help guide them.

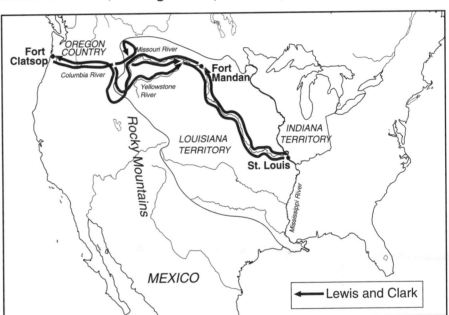

Along the way, when other Indians saw young Sacagawea with her baby, they believed the corps to be peaceful so they didn't attack. When the corps reached the mountains and needed horses to cross over them, Sacagawea convinced the Shoshone to give the men horses. When Lewis and Clark's journals almost got lost in the river, Sacagawea saved them. It was Sacagawea's people who showed the corps how to cook salmonberries and dry them for food. Sacagawea proved to be invaluable. The corps finally returned to St. Louis in September 1806.

Work in a group. Answer the questions on the back of this paper and do the activity.

1. Which rivers did the Corps of Discovery travel?

2. How long did the expedition take from leaving St. Louis until its return?

3. Did they find a direct river route from St. Louis to the Pacific? Why or why not?

Walk from your classroom to one of the locations listed below. Draw a map of your journey. Show the geography of your route. Take notes in a journal about any plants, animals, and people you see. Describe the climate and the landforms.

☐ lunchroom   ☐ library   ☐ office   ☐ swings   ☐ bus loading/unloading area

J332005 Clearly Social Studies

A YOUNG REPUBLIC

Help your students understand how the rapid growth of industry and transportation changed the way people lived in America.

Coming From Another Country

Ask your students to help you find family members and other relatives who came from another country to live in America and who would be willing to be interviewed by your class. Once a list of names is completed, have the students help you write invitations and deliver them to the would-be visitors. Assign each guest a time and date. Let the person know if he or she should bring things to share (such as traditional clothing, items from the home country, or stories about coming to America). Have the class plan a list of interview questions, such as *Which country did you come from? How is America different from your home country? Why did you leave your country? How did you feel when you first arrived in America?* For each guest, set out fresh flowers, refreshments, and a class thank-you card.

Summary Time

Transparency 5

Review for the students the events that took place during the 1700's and 1800's by displaying Transparency 5, "Historic Events Chart." Make a copy of the chart for each student. Have the students write on their charts as the class works together to fill in the transparency.

In each of the three boxes in the first column, print the name of a historical event, such as the *Industrial Revolution*, the *Invention of New Machines*, and the *Increase of Immigrants*. Have the students help you describe each event. Invite a student to record the class's ideas on the transparency as the rest of the students copy the ideas onto their own charts. Then place the students in small groups. Give each group about 10 minutes to discuss what effect each event had on America. When time is up, ask the groups for their ideas and record them on the transparency.

Crossing the Atlantic

Immigrant family's journal and pictures

After studying about the immigrants who came to America seeking a better life, place your students in "immigrant family" groups. Have each group choose a home country and write a journal that tells about their journey from their country across the Atlantic Ocean to New York Harbor. Encourage the students to include the family's feelings, fears, excitement, and hopes. Have the family groups draw pictures to illustrate their trip to America. Let each family group orally share its journal with the rest of the class. Draw and cut out the shape of a large passenger ship. Pin the ship in the center of a bulletin board. Post the journals and drawings around the ship for the rest of the school to enjoy.

 J332005 Clearly Social Studies

Building Cities

Before 1770, people made shoes, clothing, furniture, and other goods by hand in workshops and homes. By 1840, the invention of new machines changed the way

people produced goods and the way they lived. Many people moved from farms and small towns to cities, where they could work at factories and make money. People began buying factory-made goods because they didn't cost as much as handmade items. America changed from a farming or agricultural country to an industrial one. This time in history is called the "Industrial Revolution."

Eli Whitney invented the cotton gin, which helped clean up to 50 times more cotton than by hand.

As the cities became crowded, their problems grew. Cities didn't have safe sources of water and adequate sanitation. Disease and epidemics spread quickly from

unsanitary drinking water. The removal of trash was slow. In some of the poorer areas, there was little or no removal of garbage. Cities often used pigs to get rid of the garbage (although most cities had laws against hogs running freely in the streets). Cities didn't have safe neighborhoods. There wasn't enough police protection during the day and none at night. Gangs spread fear throughout neighborhoods and riots were very common. Most cities had volunteer firefighters who weren't well trained. Fires became a common, everyday occurrence.

Francis Cabot Lowell built a mill that did every stage for making cloth, from spinning the thread to weaving the cloth.

Work with a small group to create a new city. Follow the directions below.

1. List the factories and services that you will have in your city:

   ☐ fire department   ☐ police department   ☐ post office   ☐ hospital   ☐ library
   ☐ grocery store   ☐ school   ☐ other _____

2. On the back of this paper, write how you will provide the following:

   ☐ safe drinking water   ☐ good sanitation   ☐ safe environment

3. On a large sheet of butcher paper, sketch the layout of your city.

   • Draw streets and buildings. Label each one.

   • Draw parks and houses for a neighborhood.

   • Name your city. Write its population.

4. Together write a paragraph telling why your city is a good place to live.

5. Present your map and read your paragraph to the rest of the class.

J332005 Clearly Social Studies

Transportation Changes

During the 1800's, transportation in America changed. In the early 1800's, most roads were muddy, rough dirt trails. The best roads were paved with logs or rocks. Moving goods and people by wagons, stagecoaches, and horses was slow. By the mid-1800's, the government had improved the roads. A National Road built of stone and gravel joined the East with the western part of America.

The success of Robert Fulton's steam-powered boat proved that steamboats could be an efficient, fast way to move goods and people up and down rivers. The building of the 350-mile Erie Canal through much of New York made it cheaper to move goods from New York City through the Great Lakes to the West and made New York City a rich center for trade.

Because other cities wanted to be wealthy trade centers like New York City, they built canals. When their canals didn't work as well as the Erie Canal, they switched to building railroads. Transportation by train had lots of advantages. The development of steam-powered locomotives had made trains a fast way to move goods and people long distances. Trains could run wherever people built tracks. Train routes were more direct than following rivers. Tracks didn't freeze in winter like the water in canals.

Transportation played an important part in helping America grow. Canals and railroads connected the East with the ever-expanding West.

Use the information above to answer these questions. Then complete number 3.

1. Why did railroads replace canals as the best way to transport goods? Give three reasons. _____

   _____

   _____

2. Why do you think better transportation helped settle more of the West?

   _____

   _____

3. Think of how you "move" your goods—carrying your lunch from home to school or from your classroom to the lunchroom; carrying your books and homework from home to school and back. "Invent" a new machine or a new way to transport one of these goods. Draw your invention. Write how it works.

J332005 Clearly Social Studies

People Immigrate to America

From 1830 to 1850, more than 2.5 million people came to America from other countries. Thousands came from Norway, Scotland, England, Sweden, and Wales. Many more came from Ireland and Germany.

People immigrated for different reasons. Many of the Irish were poor, and after disease wiped out the potato crops that they had relied on for food, they came to America. They were starving. The Germans weren't poor but came to America to buy large, rich farmlands so that they could live a better life.

Most immigrants settled in the cities, where factory and mill owners hired men, women, and children to work the machines. Because immigrants had been so poor, they accepted low wages. Such low pay didn't help them rise above their hard life. Soon more factories were built. The housing that the owners built for the workers was cheaply constructed. Often four families lived in a tiny room in a basement without running water, heat, and light. Many children didn't go to school because they worked such long, hard hours. Immigrants also faced the anger of many native-born Americans, who were afraid they would lose their own jobs to these people who came from faraway countries and spoke foreign languages. Immigrants had a difficult life, yet they believed that their hard work would pay off.

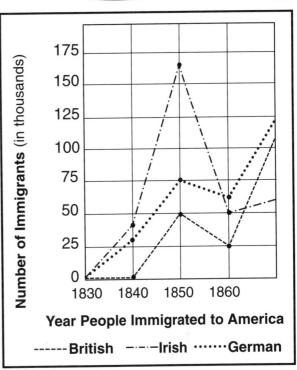

Year People Immigrated to America

------ **British** ---- **Irish** ······· **German**

Use the chart and the information to answer the questions. Then do the project.

1. In what year did the most immigrants come to America? _____

2. Which immigrants came in the largest numbers? _____

3. How many more Germans than British came in 1850? _____

4. About how many more Irish than Germans came in 1850? _____

5. In which year did 25,000 British immigrate to America? _____

PROJECT: Imagine that you are a new factory owner in the mid-1800's in America. You need to hire workers. The average wage is about 60 cents for a 10-hour day. Make a poster advertising work for hire. State what your factory makes and what it pays. Answer these questions: *Will you hire children? How will you treat your workers? Will you help immigrants who can't read, write, and speak English?* Tell about the advantages of working at your factory. Share your poster with the class.

Name _____

A Trail of Tears

As more people immigrated to America in the 1800's, many settled in the West on Native American lands. Even though America had treaties with the Indian nations stating that Indians owned the land, President Andrew Jackson believed in America's growth at all costs. Congress passed the Indian Removal Act, which allowed President Jackson to remove Native Americans from their own lands. In exchange, the Indians would receive other lands farther away. Government troops forced the Choctaw, the Chickasaw, and other Indian nations from their lands. Many who refused were taken into slavery.

The Cherokee refused to leave. Their nation was growing. They had the first Native American alphabet invented by Sequoyah, a Cherokee silversmith. Sequoyah had worked 12 years to develop this alphabet. Thousands of Cherokee men, women, and children had learned to write and read their own language. Chief John
Ross of the Cherokee nation took his case to the Supreme Court. He pleaded ". . . *Have we done any wrong? We are not charged with any. We have a Country which others covet. This is the only offense we have ever yet been charged with.*" The court ruled that the state of Georgia couldn't force the Cherokee to leave. But President Jackson thought the ruling was ridiculous and sent soldiers to arrest and round up more than 18,000 Cherokee and burn their homes. The soldiers forced men, women, and children to walk 800 miles to new lands in the West. Along the way, more than 4,000 Cherokee died from disease, starvation, and harsh treatment. This march became known as "The Trail of Tears."

Use the information above to help you do this project.

Write a letter to the President of the United States. Tell the President your opinion about the treatment of the Cherokee during the 1800's. Tell the President that you would like to erect a memorial for those thousands of Cherokee who marched in The Trail of Tears. Draw a picture of the memorial. Describe it to the President. What should it be made of? Where should it be placed? How large should it be? What words should be written on it? Be prepared to read your letter to the class.

WESTWARD, Ho!

As your students study this time in history when pioneers moved west, they will learn how "gold fever" and the desire for land fueled America's expansion.

Once Upon a Time . . .

Have each student write a short story about the day a pioneer family traveling west in a covered wagon came upon land owned by Native Americans. Tell the students to write their stories from one of these points of view—a member of the pioneer family or a member of the Lakota Sioux nation. Encourage your students to describe their characters feelings, thoughts, words, and adventures of the day when the pioneers met the Lakota. Have each student illustrate the beginning, the middle, and the end of his or her story. Have each student exchange his or her story and then read and edit the classmate's story. On another day, have each student write the final draft of his or her story. Give the students time to practice reading their stories dramatically. Let each student read his or her story to the rest of the class.

Trails Heading West

Transparency 6

Introduce the many trails of the mid-1800's that led to the West by displaying Transparency 6, "Trails Heading West, 1840's and 1850's." Tell the students that these trails were rugged and often muddy, with deep ruts from wagon wheels. Share that about 34,000 pioneers died while traveling on the Oregon Trail and that there was about one grave dug for every 100 yards of trail.

Allow students to take turns tracing with a pencil one of the trails on the transparency. Have that student try to describe some of the difficulties the pioneers might have faced along the trail based on the geography. Challenge other students to come to the overhead one at a time and ask the class a question about the map, such as *Which trail is the longest? Which trail crossed the most rivers? Which trail crossed over the most mountains?* Let that student call on other students to answer his or her question.

On the Overland Trail

200 POUNDS OF FLOUR
150 POUNDS OF BACON
10 POUNDS OF COFFEE
10 POUNDS OF SALT
20 POUNDS OF SUGAR
5 BARRELS OF WATER
CHIPPED BEEF
FRIED BEANS
RICE
DRIED FRUIT

Student group's prairie schooner and supply lists for the journey west

Remind your students that pioneers headed west for different reasons—to search for religious freedom, to escape slavery, to buy cheap land for farming, or to get rich by finding gold. Help the students form "family groups of pioneers." Have each group draw its muslin-covered prairie schooner—one that is sturdy enough for the overland journey west and can withstand river crossings. Tell the students that the typical supplies for a pioneer family in the 1840's included the following: 200 pounds of flour, 150 pounds of bacon, 10 pounds of coffee, 20 pounds of sugar, 10 pounds of salt, chipped beef, dried beans, tea, rice, and dried fruit. Have each group list its food supplies, kitchen supplies, household goods, and personal items. Have each "family member" in the group write how he or she feels about facing such a dangerous journey. Let the "families" take turns sharing their drawings, supply lists, and feelings with the rest of the class.

Days on the Trail

During the mid-1800's, thousands of families headed west. It was common to see 6,000 animals moving along with a wagon train that curved five miles long. On the trail, accidents and disease killed thousands of pioneers. Children had the most accidents. They fell out of wagons and often became lost in the crowd of hundreds of wagons and the vast frontier. Many people wrote diaries about their journeys. They wanted to record their experiences for friends and relatives who would follow later.

Read this diary excerpt written on the Oregon Trail by Lucy Henderson Deady.

 *Mother had brought some medicine along. She hung the bag containing the medicine from a nail on the side-board of the wagon. . . . My little sister, Salita Jane, wanted to taste it, but I told her she couldn't. She didn't say anything, but as soon as we had gone she got the bottle and drank it all. . . . she came to the campfire where Mother was cooking supper and said she felt sleepy. Mother told her to go away and not bother her, so she went and lay down. When Mother called her for supper she didn't come. Mother saw she was asleep, so didn't disturb her. When Mother tried to awake her later she couldn't arouse her. Lettie had drunk the whole bottle of laudanum [tincture of opium]. It was too late to save her life. . . .*

After a great hardship . . . we finally made our way . . . to Oregon . . . the winter rains had started. We had been eight months on the road . . . we were out of food, and our cattle were nearly worn out. . . . My mother's brother came out and met us. We left the wagons and with mother on one horse holding her 6 week old baby in her lap, and with one of the little children sitting behind her and with the rest of us riding behind the different men, we started north . . . There were five of us children. . . . We lived on boiled wheat and boiled peas that winter. . . .

1. What do you think Lucy was trying to tell other pioneer families? _____
   _____

2. What kind of qualities do you think a pioneer child should have to survive?
   _____
   _____

3. If your family was heading west, what would you ask Lucy? Write five questions.
   _____
   _____
   _____
   _____
   _____

Compare and contrast,
Application

The Rush for a Better Life

Thousands rushed to California in 1849 searching for gold. These early settlers were called "Forty-Niners" because that was the year when "Gold Rush fever" was at its peak. Gold seekers took over land owned by Native Americans and fought amongst themselves over who owned what land. California grew rapidly. Soon merchants, barbers, doctors, and lawyers came. All were in search of a better life like the pioneers.

List what is similar and different about the two pictures. Write your answer to the question on the back of this paper.

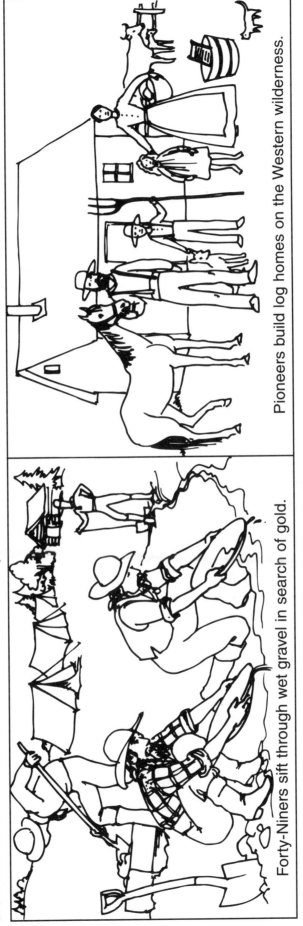

Forty-Niners sift through wet gravel in search of gold.

Pioneers build log homes on the Western wilderness.

Similarities: _____

Differences: _____

If you were an adult living during the Gold Rush, would you want to be a pioneer or a "Forty-Niner"? Why?

J332005 Clearly Social Studies

Name _____

Moving on to Native American Lands

As pioneers moved into the West, Native Americans were forced to sell or give up their ancient lands. Thousands of Native Americans lost their lands and their freedom. During this time, Chief Seattle (the leader of groups of Northwest Coast Indians) guided white settlers and traded with them. But in 1854, when the United States government forced more of his people from their land, Chief Seattle spoke out against it and refused to sign a land treaty.

Read the excerpts from Chief Seattle's famous speech. Then answer the questions.

Every shining pine needle, every sandy shore, every mist in the dark woods, every clearing and humming insect is holy in the memory and experience of my people. Teach your children what we have taught our children, that the Earth is our mother. The rivers are our brothers, they quench our thirst and feed our children. The air is precious to the red man, for all things share the same breath—the beast, the tree, the man, they all share the same breath. And what is man without the beasts? . . .

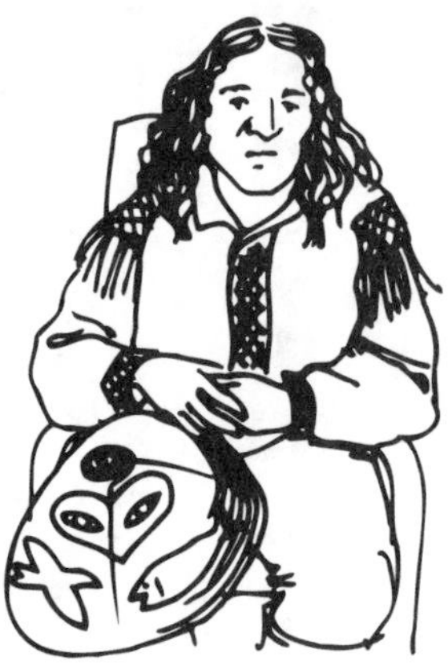

This we know. The Earth does not belong to man; man belongs to the Earth. Man did not weave the web of life, he is merely a strand in it. Whatever he does to the web, he does to himself. All things are connected like the blood which unites one family. . . . . . . How can you buy or sell the sky? The land? . . .

1. Why does Chief Seattle say that air is precious? _____

_____

2. Why does Chief Seattle say the rivers are our brothers? _____

_____

3. How would you answer Chief Seattle's question: *What is man without the beasts?* _____

_____

4. Do you agree with Chief Seattle that Earth doesn't belong to us, but we belong to Earth? Why or why not? _____

_____

_____

_____

5. *Whatever we do to the web of life, we do to ourselves.* Write what you think this means on the back of this paper. Draw a picture to illustrate your answer.

War with Mexico

In the 1820's, thousands of Americans rushed to settle in Texas. Land was cheap. Most of it was free! It was also owned by Mexico. Within 10 years, the immigrants outnumbered the Mexicans. As a result, Mexico put a stop to American immigration. This angered Texans. They fought the Mexican army and won their independence. Later, when Texas became part of the United States, the border between Texas and Mexico was always in question. This problem led to a war between the U.S. and Mexico. At the end of the Mexican War, the U.S. paid Mexico $15 million dollars for the land it received and later paid another $10 million for more Mexican-owned land.

This map shows the U.S. lands gained from Mexico. Follow the directions below.

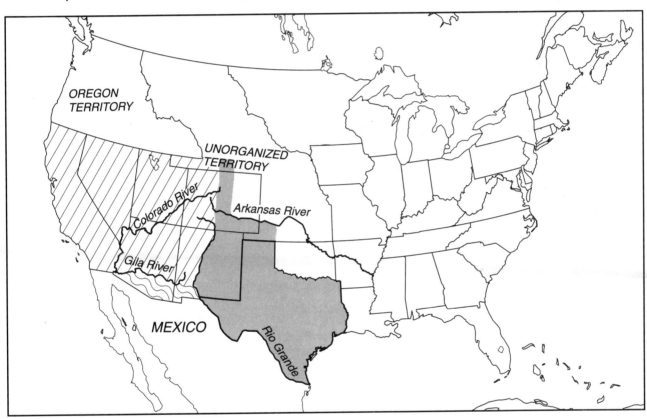

1. In 1845, Texas became part of the United States. Label **Texas**. The ▨ dotted area shows all the land acquired at that time. Color that land yellow.

2. The diagonal lines show land that the United States bought from Mexico in 1848, after the Mexican War. This is the land of six states: **California**, **Nevada**, **Utah**, **Arizona**, **Colorado**, and **New Mexico**. Label them. Color this land green.

3. The wavy lines show land that the United States bought from Mexico in 1853. Color it orange. How many years was this from the last purchase? _____

4. How did the Mexican War change the U.S.? Write on the back of this paper.

A FUTURE FOR AMERICA

Help your students appreciate the struggles of the many different people who helped build a better America and fought for liberty and equality.

Using a Flow Chart

Transparency 7

Help your students discover how one event in history flows into another and another until eventually a major change occurs. First, display Transparency 7, "Flow Chart." Reproduce a flow chart for each student to complete while you model how to fill in information on the transparency. Start by choosing a historic event such as the building of the transcontinental railroad. Ask the students to think of other events that happened as a result of that main event. Challenge your students to write a related event in each shape on the chart, ending with the cumulative historic change or event.

Repeat this activity by personalizing it. Have each student think of an event in his or her life. Then tell the students to list other life events that resulted from that first event. Give the students a chance to share their personal flow charts with the class.

Getting the Main Idea

Transparency 8

After reading about a historic event, display Transparency 8, "Main Idea Map." Reproduce a copy of the map for each student. Decide as a class what the main idea or topic is and guide the students to think of three subtopics. Have students write a detailed description for each subtopic. This map activity is a great way to review information.

Challenge the students by asking them to answer a question such as *How did African American slaves finally gain freedom?* Place the students in small groups and have each group complete a main idea map to answer the question. Tell each group to write the question in the center rectangle. Then prompt the students by asking: *What are three events that helped slaves gain freedom? Can you describe what took place during each event?* Give each group time to read aloud its information and display its map.

A group's monument to liberty

Monuments for Liberty

It is only with the heart that one can see rightly;
What is essential is invisible to the eye —
Antoine de Saint Exupéry

Lead a class discussion about the meaning of *liberty, freedom,* and *independence.* Write them on a white board and let different students tell what these words mean to them. Remind the students of how long and hard colonists, African American slaves, immigrants, and women fought for their equal rights of freedom, liberty, and independence. Place your students into small groups. Have each group design and draw a monument to liberty on large butcher paper. Let each group do research to find a quote to write on the base of its monument. Have the groups cut out their finished monuments and display them. Let the groups take turns explaining their monuments and reading their quotes. Invite another class to listen.

Name _____

The Struggle to End Slavery

After Abraham Lincoln became President of the United States, the Civil War began between the North and the South. The southern states left, or seceded from, the Union to form their own country. They wanted to keep their way of life and their right to own slaves. The North didn't need slaves. Some northerners formed anti-slavery, or abolitionist, groups. Read about three people who worked to end slavery.

Harriet Tubman was born a slave in Maryland. At 29, she escaped to the North but had to leave behind her family. While escaping, Tubman promised herself that ". . . No man should take me alive. I should fight for my liberty as long as my strength lasted." Tubman wanted to get her family. She was determined that her "people must go free." Later, she risked her life to work as a conductor on the Underground Railroad— and helped more than 300 slaves escape to the North.

During the Civil War, she worked for the Union.

Frederick Douglass was born a slave in Maryland. His owner's wife taught him to read. At 21, Douglass escaped to the North. He spoke against slavery and found that his speeches had the power to inspire. He was hired to speak all over the country. In a speech he said, "[Why should I have] to argue that it is wrong to make men brutes, to rob them of their liberty, . . . to sell them at auction . . ." Douglass also started *The North Star,* an anti-slavery newspaper.

During the Civil War, he recruited African Americans for the Union Army.

Abraham Lincoln was born a free man in Kentucky. He was the 16th President of the United States. He wanted to keep the country united, to keep the North free, and to let slavery die out in the South. He said, "A house divided against itself cannot stand. I believe this government cannot endure, permanently half slave and half free." In 1863, Lincoln issued the Emancipation Proclamation, which said all slaves in the U.S. were free. "What I do about slavery, I do because . . . it helps to save this Union." In 1865, the North won the war and slavery ended.

Answer these questions on the back of this paper.

1. Both Douglass and Lincoln had power to help end slavery. How was their power the same? How was it different?

2. Both Tubman and Douglass escaped slavery. They both risked their lives to help free other slaves. How was their bravery the same? How was it different?

3. What do you think would have happened if slave hunters had caught Tubman?

4. Why do you think Douglass recruited African Americans to join the Union army?

5. What did Lincoln mean by "a house divided against itself cannot stand"?

6. Out of the three persons, whom do you think was the most courageous? Why?

Name _____

Making a New Life in America

After the Civil War, millions of immigrants from Europe and Asia sailed to America. New inventions, which helped make goods faster and cheaper, led to the building of factories where unskilled immigrants found work. The transcontinental railroad, linking California with the East, allowed thousands of immigrants to move west. The building of more railroads gave jobs to Japanese, Irish, and Chinese immigrants as well as Mexican American migrants. Read about the lives of some immigrants. Answer the questions on the back of this paper.

We are from Ireland. I am 11. My brother is 10. I work 12 hours a day cutting threads from cloth. I get $1.50 each week. My brother works in a coal mine. The money helps our family. Every day for lunch we eat a pickle and a piece of bread.

I brought my family from China. At our little shop we sell Chinese food—mushrooms, tea, ginger, and cabbage. We cannot speak or read English well. American money is confusing. We make many mistakes. But we are learning!

My family lives near my uncle and his family. Our neighbors are all from Italy. We speak Italian and eat special foods. The whole street celebrates Italian holidays! America is a good home for us.

My family is poor. We must live in a crowded building in the big, dirty city. I work six days a week for $10.00. My 9-year-old son sells newspapers.

1. How did the transcontinental railroad help the immigrants?

2. Why do you think factories hired so many children?

3. What were some of the hardships that immigrants faced? List at least four.

4. Why do you think that immigrants settled in neighborhoods with other families from their home country?

5. Why do you think that America finally passed a law that said children had to be 16 years old to work at most jobs?

6. Imagine that you are a factory owner in 1872. Who would you hire? What kinds of working conditions would you have for the immigrants who worked for you?

J332005 Clearly Social Studies

Fighting for the Right to Vote

Throughout American history, brave people have tried to correct social injustices in different ways—writing letters and articles, holding meetings, giving speeches, introducing amendments, organizing movements, and purposely breaking an unjust law. For more than 100 years, many people fought to give women the right to vote. Read about these methods in the flow chart below. Then do one of the projects.

In 1778, Hannah Lee Corbin writes a letter to Richard Henry Lee and asks him to help women win the right to vote. He is her brother and a political leader of that time. Her letter receives no action.

In 1848, Lucretia Mott and Elizabeth Cady Stanton organize a meeting at Seneca Falls, New York. More than 300 women attend and speak about women's right to vote. Stanton reads a changed version of the Declaration of Independence that says . . . *all men **and women** are created equal.*

In 1872, Susan B. Anthony and others meet in Rochester, New York. Claiming their right to vote, they vote in an election. Anthony is arrested and fined $100!

In 1869, women's suffrage (right to vote) gets its first real victory. The Wyoming Territory becomes the first part of the United States to give women the right to vote.

The meeting at Seneca Falls starts political leaders thinking about women's suffrage.

In 1878, a senator brings up a suffrage amendment in Congress. It's voted down. But supporters begin calling for the "Anthony Amendment."

In 1920, the 19th Amendment is ratified. It gives women the right to vote.

Votes for Women!

Be ready to share your project with the class!

☐ Imagine you are a reporter in 1920. Prepare a special report about the new 19th Amendment. Describe it and tell why it's important to America. Give the highlights of its history. Present your report as a radio news reporter.

☐ Imagine that your school district has proposed that students attend school on Saturdays. As a student, you do not have the right to vote on this issue. Write how you will help convince the principal, the parents, and the school board that students should have the right to vote on this proposal. Present your plan to the class.

Project deadline: _____

J332005 Clearly Social Studies

Symbols of America

The bald eagle isn't bald! It looks that way because of the white feathers on its head. The eagle is a symbol of strength, skill, and bravery. In 1782, Congress chose the bald eagle as a national symbol. (Benjamin Franklin suggested the turkey!) Bald eagles only live in North America. They are an endangered species and must be protected.

The Statue of Liberty was declared a national monument in 1924. It was a gift from France to celebrate America's first 100 years. This 151-foot copper statue was designed by a French sculptor named Bartholdi. It is a symbol of hope and freedom for immigrants coming to America. "Miss Liberty" stands on Liberty Island in New York Harbor.

This flag is a national symbol for America. Its most popular name is "Stars and Stripes." It has 50 stars, one for each state, on a blue background and 13 red and white stripes for the original 13 colonies. The flag stands for the land, the people, the government, and America's ideals. It also stands for hope, honor, and courage.

The Great Seal of the United States is stamped on or attached to important papers and letters from the president. No other country in the world uses this red, white, and blue seal. The arrows the eagle holds stand for the ability to wage war. It also holds an olive branch, which stands for the desire for peace. The Eye of Providence stands for God.

front

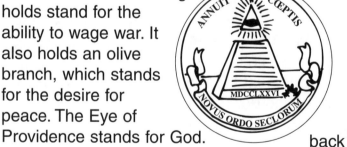

back

Work in a group. Do one project below. Be ready to share your project with the class.

☐ Design a new American symbol to be used by students. Tell how it compares to one of the existing symbols. Describe what it stands for and its significance.

☐ Write and perform a song or poem about one of America's symbols.

☐ Draw a large banner showing the important symbols of America. Write a few sentences below each symbol describing its significance.

Protecting Our Democracy

Democracy comes from two Greek words—
demos, which means "people," and *kratos*, which
means "power." The United States government is a
democracy. Its power comes from the people. More
than 200 years ago, the writers of the Constitution
created the government and the rules the
government must follow. They established three
branches of government so that no one branch
would become too powerful. Later, a Bill of Rights
was added. It lists the basic freedoms that all
American citizens are entitled to claim, such as the right to choose your own religion
and the right to speak openly.

Throughout America's history, ordinary people have worked hard to protect our
freedoms and rights. Groups of Americans have worked to win a woman's right to
vote, to get equal pay for women doing the same jobs as men, to give equal
opportunities to disabled people, and to have equal rights and pay for African
Americans, Native Americans, and migrant workers.

There are certain rights that you enjoy at your school—the right to ask questions and
the freedom to choose what you want to play at recess. With a group, read and talk
about the meaning of these two verses of "America the Beautiful." It was written by
Samuel Ward and Katherine Lee Bates. Then follow the directions below.

America the Beautiful

O beautiful for spacious skies,
For amber waves of grain,
For purple mountain majesties,
Above the fruited plain!
America! America!
God shed His grace on thee.
And crown thy good with brotherhood
From sea to shining sea!

O beautiful for heroes proved
In liberating strife,
Who more than self their country loved,
And mercy more than life!
America! America!
May God thy gold refine,
Till all success be nobleness,
And ev'ry gain divine!

1. One way to protect your rights at school
   is to write a school song honoring them.
   This way you can remind students of
   their rights. With your group, list the
   freedoms and rights that you have as a
   student at your school. List some of the
   best things about your school.

2. Use your list to write two verses of a
   song that honors the rights and
   freedoms you enjoy as a student. Use
   the melody to "America the Beautiful" or
   choose another patriotic song.

3. Write your verses on a large sheet of
   butcher paper. Illustrate your words
   along the song's borders.

4. Sing your song to the rest of the class!

J332005 Clearly Social Studies

ANSWERS

Page 6
1. The first people migrated to northwestern North America because 28,000 B.C. is before 17,000 B.C.
2. 3,000 years
3. 19,000 years

Page 7
1. SW
2. NW
3. NW
4. both
5. SW
6. NW
7. NW
8. SW
9. SW
10. NW

Answer varies. Possible answer: Both groups learned to live off of their environment.

Page 8
Wording varies. Possible answers:
1. Dogs pulled the Indians' supplies for them.
2. Tepees were portable. They were warm in winter and cool in summer.
3. The horse let the Indians hunt farther and faster.
4. The Indians hadn't been exposed to those diseases before.
5. Answer varies.

Page 9
1. Woodland Indians lived among large <u>forests</u> and <u>lakes</u>.
2. They often picked <u>wild</u> <u>rice</u>, which grew beside the water.
3. Some tribes farmed <u>corn, squash,</u> and <u>beans</u>.
4. <u>Iroquoian</u> and <u>Algonquian</u> were the two main languages.
5. Bark-covered Iroquois homes were called <u>longhouses</u>.
6. The Algonquin wigwams were made from bent <u>willow</u> <u>poles</u>.
7. The leaders of the clans were called the <u>clan</u> <u>mothers</u>.
8. The groups shared a lot yet they fought over <u>trade</u> and <u>land</u>.

BONUS: Project varies.

Page 13
A. Hudson
B. Drake
C. Cartier
D. Da Gama
E. Dias
F. Columbus
Answers vary.

Page 14
Wording varies. Possible answers:
1. The French controlled the Mississippi, Missouri, and Arkansas rivers.
2. Cortés, Coronado, and Oñate helped create New Spain. (Could include Pizarro)
3. Answer varies. Possible answer: The Spanish explored more land because they traveled through Central and South America.
4. Answer varies. Possible answers: France and Spain wanted colonies in the Americas to build their own countries, to get rich by trading with Native Americans, to become more powerful.
   France and Spain didn't explore the West because the land was rugged, mountainous, and difficult to explore.

Page 15
Wording varies. Possible answers:
1. The people sent the Spanish king part of the gold and silver mined by the Indians.
2. The French missionaries lived with the Indians to try to convert them. They didn't force the Indians to live and work in the missions.
3. New France sold furs that they had traded with the Indians.
4. The French trading posts later grew into cities.
5. Answer varies. Possible answer: It seems that the Spanish brought more negative effects to the Americas by forcing Indians to live and work in missions and change their way of life and beliefs. They also brought Africans to the Americas to work as slaves. They brought many diseases, which killed the Indians.

Page 18
Student completes a map of 13 colonies and their products.

Page 19
Wording may vary for outline.
I. There were reasons that Jamestown was to be built.
   A. The colonists were to give the merchants a share of gold and crops.
   B. The colonists had a plan to get rich quick and return to England.
II. There were advantages in settling by a river.
   A. The river would protect the men from Indian attacks.
   B. They could escape on the river.
   C. They carried goods up and down the river.
   D. The river gave them fish, wildlife and fresh water.
III. There were disadvantages in settling by a river.
   A. At high tide the ocean spilled into the river and contaminated it.
   B. The water made the land swampy.
   C. Mosquitoes carried deadly diseases.
IV. Captain John Smith helped Jamestown succeed.
   A. He ruled that those who didn't work, didn't eat.
   B. He forced the men to build, to hunt, and to farm.
   C. He traded with the Powhatan for food.

Page 20

	Length of Time Required to Work for Someone	Rights They Had	Choices They Were Given	Land They Could Own	When They Could Gain Freedom
Indentured Servant	up to 7 years	were given freedom, clothing, and land	could go to other colonies to work	were given land when debt was paid	when debt was paid
American Indian	life	none with white people	none — except escape	none	when they escaped
African Slave	life	none	none	none	none

Answer to question varies. Possible answer: The indentured servant had the "better" life because he or she had a choice of even becoming a worker. Once the indentured servant worked off his or her debt, the person was free and was given land to own. This person had rights and choices.

Page 21
Answers may vary.
1. Farming was difficult because of the thin, rocky soil.
2. Families did chores, studied, and ate in the "keeping room."
3. Children were taught to read so they could read the Bible.
4. No. Puritans believed that only male church members should govern.
5. People who believed differently than the Puritans left their colonies and settled in other ones or started their own colonies. This way New England could develop and grow with people sharing a variety of beliefs.

ANSWERS

Page 22
1. 43°N
2. 74°W
3. 74°W
4. Dover
5. New York
6. Susquehanna River
7. 41°N

Questions vary.

Page 23
Answers vary. Possible answers:
1. If the hired workers on the Mayflower did not sign the Mayflower Compact, there would have been dissension within the Pilgrim colony of Plymouth. Perhaps these workers would have traveled on their own to Virginia and not helped build Plymouth. The Pilgrims might not have survived at all that first winter!
2. William Bradford and William Penn are similar in many ways. They are both from England and both broke away from the Church of England. They both feared being put in prison. They both believed in living in a place where people could worship freely. They both believed in self-government for the colonies. Through their leadership, the colonies made peace with the Indians in the area. They were both Christians.
   William Bradford was a Pilgrim and William Penn was a Quaker.

Page 26
Wording may vary. Possible answers:
1. They wanted colonies because they were making money from selling American furs and fish.
2. France built forts to stop the British from moving west.
3. The British sent soldiers to remove them.
4. The French were outnumbered by the British soldiers.
5. The French and the Indians joined together to fight against the British.
6. Great Britain owned more land in America and was in great debt, France lost land, the Indians lost power, and the colonists gained self-confidence.

Page 27
Answers vary. Possible answers:
1. The colonists were forced to pay taxes because Britain had drained its treasury.
2. Parliament lowered the tax on molasses but didn't repeal it.
3. The men formed the "Sons of Liberty" and the women formed the "Daughters of Liberty."
4. The colonists boycotted any goods imported from Britain.
5. Parliament repealed the Townshend Acts because of the colonial boycott.
6. Perhaps Britain kept its tax on tea because so many colonists drank tea, a tradition which they brought with them from England to America.
7. Answer varies. Possible answer: The colonists were so effective against British taxes because they united together in protests and boycotts. They were more powerful by uniting.

Page 30
Answer varies. Possible answer:
   Paul Revere and Sybil Ludington had much in common. They both lived during the time of the American Revolution, and they were both for independence. Both of them rode on horseback at midnight to warn the colonists of the attacking British soldiers. They both rode from farm to farm. They both patted their horses to reassure and comfort the animals. Both of them showed great courage.
   Paul Revere and Sybil Ludington have differences also. Revere was a lot older than 16 when he rode to warn of the advancing British soldiers. Ludington came upon thieves and escaped. She also did this 40-mile journey because her father was a commander of the colonial soldiers. Revere is most famous because of Longfellow's historic poem. Most people don't know about Sybil Ludington's brave ride.

Page 31
Answers vary.

Page 32
Loyalists
Before the War: lived side by side with patriots
During and After the War: treated badly, had homes and property taken away, left America

Colonial Women
Before the War: tended gardens, made clothes, cared for house and children
During and After the War: told farm workers what to do, ran flour mills and shops, paid bills, managed money

African American Volunteers
Before the War: slaves
During and After the War: freedom, left America, found jobs

Indians who aided British
Before the War: lived on own land, set up treaties with colonists
During and After the War: villages burned, crops destroyed, land taken away, many moved to Canada

Page 33
Answers vary. Possible answers:
1. agree; The Congress sent the king an offering of peace.
2. disagree; By rejecting this chance for peace, the king ended up fighting a long war and lost the colonies.
3. agree; He wrote the Declaration.
4. disagree; The king thought of the men as traitors.
5. Answer varies.

Page 34

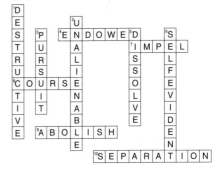

ANSWERS

Page 35

Answers vary. Possible answers:

1. It took 4 years for the Bill of Rights to be added to the Constitution.
2. Each state made its own laws, collected its own taxes, and made its own money. These important powers belonged to the states instead of to the central government.
3. The Northwest Ordinance outlawed slavery and established the rights of citizens.
4. The legislative branch makes the laws and collects the taxes. The executive branch is headed by the president and enforces the laws. The judicial branch decides the meaning of the laws.
5. The Bill of Rights describes the basic rights of each citizen and protects those rights. Individual rights were not addressed in the Constitution.

Page 36

Answers vary. Possible answers:

1. (Child's drawings are different. Biography art should be more serious than the tall tale art.)
2. adventure in his blood; shoot a beaver that was five miles away while blindfolded and backwards; with one shot, he knocked that buffalo to the ground; he didn't get one scratch; Boone just grinned so big at the chief that the sun bounced off of his teeth and lit up the forest like it was on fire
3. A biography tries to stay as close to the truth as possible. A tall tale tries to exaggerate the truth.
4. Daniel Boone was born in 1734; his Quaker family; North Carolina frontier; learned to shoot and hunt; captured by the Shawnee; Shawnee adopted him

Page 37

1. Missouri River, Columbia River, Yellowstone River
2. two years and 4 months
3. They didn't find a direct river route to the Pacific because the Rocky Mountains divided the land and rivers.

Page 40

Answers vary. Possible answers:

1. Steam-powered trains were a fast way to move goods and people long distances. Train routes were more direct than following rivers. Trains could run in the winter.

Trains were faster than horse-drawn canal boats.

2. People and goods could be transported more easily and faster to the West. Transportation connected the East and the West.

Page 41

1. 1850
2. Irish
3. 25,000 more
4. About 85,000 more
5. 1860

Page 44

Answers vary. Possible answers:

1. Keep careful watch over your young children. Place your medicines in a locked container. Life is harsh and dangerous.
2. A pioneer child should use common sense, eat healthy, be cautious, stay in view of family, be brave, be truthful, and always have hope.
3. Questions vary.

Page 45

Answers vary. Possible answers:
Similarities:
    rugged people, hard workers, lived on land, depended on land, hardy
Differences:
    pioneers lived in families and most miners were men, pioneers lived in houses and miners lived in tents, pioneers had pets and miners didn't

Page 46

Answers vary. Possible answers:

1. Air is precious because we all share it with the animals.
2. Rivers give us water to drink.
3. If the animals died, people wouldn't be able to survive.
4. I agree that we belong to Earth because we live on the planet. We are just a part of it like the plants and animals.
5. Whatever we do to Earth—pollute it, care for it, restore its endangered plants and animals—we affect all of life on Earth.

Page 47

3. 5 years
4. Answer varies. Possible answer: The United States expanded to the Pacific Ocean because of the Mexican War. The United States reached from the Atlantic to the Pacific. It also expanded southward into Mexico.

Page 49

Answers vary. Possible answers:

1. Both Douglass and Lincoln had power in inspiring people by their speeches. Both became famous leaders, which gave them power. Douglass had power through his words to help end slavery; whereas Lincoln had the power to create laws to end slavery.
2. Tubman and Douglass were brave in how they escaped slavery. Both were brave in speaking out against slavery. Tubman was brave in risking her life to help slaves on the Underground Railroad; whereas Douglass was brave with his words as he gave speeches to convince people to be against slavery.
3. If Tubman got caught trying to escape slavery, she probably would have fought against the slave catchers until they killed her. Her words seem to mean that she'd rather be dead than a slave.
4. Douglass recruited African Americans to join the Union Army because the Union stood for free states. He wanted the North to win the war, and thus end slavery.
5. "A house divided against itself cannot stand" probably meant that a country not united and fighting against each other would eventually fall apart.
6. Answer varies.

Page 50

Answers vary. Possible answers:

1. The transcontinental railroad made it easier for immigrants to move into the West.
2. Factories hired children because they could pay them low wages for long hours of work.
3. Immigrants had to live in crowded places, had trouble with English, didn't know the money system, and had to have their children work to help out the family.
4. Immigrants settled together so they could speak their native language, eat special foods, and celebrate together.
5. Young children should go to school and not work.
6. Answer varies.